SILENT
WITNESS

ALSO BY MARK FUHRMAN

Murder in Brentwood
Murder in Spokane
Murder in Greenwich
Death and Justice

SILENT
WITNESS

The Untold Story of
Terri Schiavo's Death

Mark Fuhrman

WM

WILLIAM MORROW
An Imprint of HarperCollinsPublishers

Insert photographs courtesy of the Schindler family.

HarperCollins books may be purchased for educational, business, or sales promotional use. For information please write: Special Markets Department, HarperCollins Publishers, 10 East 53rd Street, New York, NY 10022.

FIRST EDITION

Printed on acid-free paper

Library of Congress Cataloging-in-Publication Data has been applied for.

ISBN 0-06-085337-9

05 06 07 08 09 WBC / RRD 10 9 8 7 6 5 4 3 2 1

For Terri Schiavo

Contents

CONTENTS

Acknowledgments

This book was written in a very short period of time. The following people made it possible.

Stephen Weeks—my partner and friend who cannot be replaced.

Sean Hannity—the man who got me involved.

Bob and Mary Schindler—who opened their home and hearts.

Bobby Schindler—for his painful memories and honesty.

Suzanne Vitadamo—for her strength.

Michael Vitadamo—for the pizza. Yo Vito!

Pamela Hennessey—for her countless hours documenting the case.

Pat Anderson—for her legal mind and quick wit.

Tom Broderson—for all his help.

David Gibbs and Barbara Weller—for their generous assistance.

Kelly Fisher—my girlfriend, who provided medical information and care packages.

George McClane—for bringing the medicine down to my level.

Michael Baden—for always being there for me when I need him.

Al Lowman—my agent who always comes through.

KGA Radio—for letting me take the time from my show.

Rebecca Mack—my producer, who took the helm in my absence.

Lynda Bensky—a great agent.

Meaghan Dowling—a great editor.

Rome Quezada—for all his hard work.

Gabriel Coltrane Weeks—for being cute.

Pascale Charbon—for taking care of Gabe.

Introduction

When I first heard of Terri Schiavo, it seemed that a grieving and caring husband was trying desperately to carry out the wishes of his comatose wife.

That was 2003, when her feeding tube had been removed for the second time.

From then on, the Terri Schiavo story was presented in the media through the perspective of a debate over euthanasia, dominated by talking heads representing various advocacy groups making predictable arguments about the "right to life" and "right to die." Almost everybody seemed to overlook the fact that nobody knew why Terri had collapsed fifteen years earlier.

The case proceeded along the official channels until all legal means were exhausted and the feeding tube of Terri Schiavo was removed for the third time on March 18, 2005. Emergency appeals, and even Mary Schindler's plea to Michael Schiavo to let her daughter live, fell on deaf ears.

While Terri was starving to death, President Bush requested that Congress meet in a special session to pass a law and hopefully save her life. Congressmen and senators rushed back from their vacation homes to debate the bill, which was passed after a heated partisan argument and lots of overblown rhetoric on both sides.

President Bush flew back from his ranch in Crawford, Texas, to sign the bill in Washington.

I couldn't believe what Congress and the president had done. I may not be a constitutional-law scholar, but it appeared to me that the federal government was trying to override Florida state law and the courts to save one person's life. I'm all in favor of saving innocent lives, but you have to do it by following the law, not rewriting it to fit one individual case. Even more offensive was the politicians' obvious motivation to capitalize on Terri's suffering and her family's misery.

Both Republicans and Democrats were guilty of politicizing a human tragedy. The Republicans showed themselves to be more interested in the opportunity to express their support of the "right to life" than to actually save one. And the Democrats were more concerned with the abstract issue of the "right to die" than with the fact that a state circuit court had ordered an innocent woman to die of starvation and dehydration, and the appellate courts were giving her less constitutional protection than a convicted murderer.

To many of the politicians and advocacy groups, Terri Schiavo was a poster child for their cause, not someone's daughter or wife. Florida senator Mel Martinez's memo, passed to his colleagues on the Senate floor, described the Terri Schiavo case as a "great political issue," which might help the Republican Party in upcoming elections. That's funny; I didn't see this as a political issue. I saw a mother trying desperately to save her daughter's life and a husband trying to end it.

After the Senate compromise bill was passed, the American people were asked what they thought, and they spoke loud and clear. Eighty-two percent of Americans polled by CBS News disagreed with Congress and the president's intervention in the case.

Then Terri Schiavo died. And all of a sudden it was no longer an abstract issue, but the loss of a human life, however diminished by injury. Most people expected the story to end. For me, it was only beginning.

A few days after Terri died, Sean Hannity called me at home. Sean had just spent a week in Florida covering the countdown to Terri's death. He had grown close to the Schindler family, who had been begging law enforcement agencies to look into charges that Michael Schiavo had abused Terri, and not getting anywhere. Sean asked me, "Will you investigate this case?" Sean went on for the better part of an hour about the case, the evidence, and what his gut was telling him.

"I don't care what you find," Sean told me. "I just want to know what happened to her."

By the time the phone call ended, we both agreed that I should write this book.

My approach seemed clear. Concentrate on the time of Terri's injury and answer the questions that had never even been asked. How did this young woman collapse? Was there any criminality? Had she possibly been abused or even murdered?

I thought I could remain safely above the highly charged emotional issues simply by playing a detached detective. Once I arrived in Florida and began researching the case, however, I realized that this would be impossible.

I am not a religious man. As a homicide detective, I learned to develop a clinical perspective concerning life and death. Sometimes that's enough to block out the pain you see in others. Sometimes it's not.

Before I sat down and spoke with Mary Schindler, I did not understand how dedicated a mother's love could be. There was no hope that Terri would ever be the woman she had once been. That didn't matter to Mary Schindler. Terri's father, Bob, was racked with pain and anger and guilt. Here was a man whose little girl had been starved to death by a court order while he stood by helpless and watched.

Very quickly I found that my police experience could not prepare me for the issues in this case that go beyond the question of how Terri Schiavo died. It took fifteen years for her to die, and that death didn't resolve anything or provide any closure. The sadness and pain are still raw, and the questions that this case raised about life and death and love and hate will haunt me for a long time. My challenge in this book is to investigate Terri's collapse and her subsequent death using the same detective tools I would in any other case—the timeline, witness statements, medical evidence—without forgetting that her death affected us all, in ways we don't even yet realize.

CHAPTER ONE

Fourteen Days to Die

FRIDAY, MARCH 18, 2005

"I felt like Terri was finally going to get what she wants, and be at peace and be with the Lord."

— MICHAEL SCHIAVO

"I'm begging you, don't let my daughter die."

— MARY SCHINDLER

At 1:45 P.M. Terri Schiavo's gastric feeding tube is removed, following a court order. Schiavo, a forty-one-year-old female, collapsed in her home on February 25, 1990, and suffered severe brain damage because of lack of oxygen to the brain. The precise cause of her collapse remains unknown, although there is speculation that it was the result of a potassium imbalance caused by an eating disorder.

Terri is being cared for at Hospice House Woodside in Pinellas Park, Florida. It is expected that she will die within seven to fourteen days. Courts have ruled that Terri is in a "persistent vegetative state," meaning that damage to her cerebral cortex has rendered her incapable of emotion, memory, or thought. This diagnosis is contested by her parents and siblings, the Schindlers.

Her husband, Michael Schiavo, has argued that Terri would not have wanted to be kept alive in her current condition. Although Terri had left no written instructions on whether or not she wished her life to be terminated in such a condition, a court has accepted testimony from her husband and in-laws that she told them she would not want to be kept alive if incapacitated.

The legal struggle between Schiavo and the Schindlers has lasted more than twelve years, with courts consistently ruling in the husband's favor. This is the third time the feeding tube has been removed.

Michael Schiavo has two children with his fiancée, Jodi Centonze. If he divorces Terri, he loses custody of her. The guardianship and her estate would be inherited by her immediate family, who have said they would keep her alive. Michael has been in a relationship with Centonze since 1995. Since 1993, the Schindlers have asked Michael to divorce Terri, give up custody, and let them take responsibility for her care. He has always refused.

"Michael and Jodi, you have your own children. Please, please give my child back to me."

— MARY SCHINDLER

"The courts have repeatedly said, this case is not about Mrs. Schindler, Mr. Schiavo or any other third party. It's about Mrs. Schiavo and her own wishes not to be kept alive artificially."

— GEORGE FELOS, ATTORNEY FOR MICHAEL SCHIAVO

The removal of Terri's feeding tube creates a political firestorm. A congressional committee issues subpoenas commanding Terri and Michael Schiavo, along with physicians and other hospice personnel, to appear before them. The committee also moves to intervene in the guardianship case between Schiavo and the Schindlers, and asks circuit-court judge George Greer to stay his order requiring the removal of the feeding tube. Greer denies both motions. The committee's appeals go as high as the U.S. Supreme Court, and are all denied. The Schindlers file a petition for habeas corpus, the same procedure used for prisoners awaiting execution, in the federal district court. Their petition is dismissed.

> *"Certainly an incapacitated person deserves at least the same protection afforded criminals sentenced to death."*
>
> — FLORIDA GOVERNOR JEB BUSH

Shortly after her feeding tube is removed, Terri Schiavo receives the Catholic ceremony of last rites. Michael Schiavo stays in a room down the hall. He remains at his wife's side throughout the day, except when her immediate family comes to see Terri. Visiting schedules at the hospice are arranged so that Michael Schiavo and the Schindlers do not see one another. The family spends their time in a thrift shop converted into a temporary headquarters across the street from the hospice. Protesters, most of them supporting the Schindlers, begin gathering outside the hospice.

SATURDAY, MARCH 19

Police stand guard around the hospice to ensure that no one attempts to give Terri food or water. Barricades are set up on the street. The Schindlers have to pass three separate checkpoints, where they are searched and their IDs are verified, before they are allowed into Terri's room. They can visit only when Michael allows them to, and are not given fixed visiting hours. When they are not allowed to visit, the police will not tell them when to come back and try again. Several days later, the police decided to come over to the thrift shop to let them know when they could visit. Once inside the room, they are forbidden to take photographs or videos of Terri.

"It was horrible. We were treated like common criminals."

—ROBERT SCHINDLER, TERRI'S FATHER

"It was like we shouldn't be there. We were doing something wrong."

—SUZANNE VITADAMO, TERRI'S SISTER

Delaying its Easter recess, the U.S. Senate convenes to give formal permission to the House of Representatives to return to session and draft legislation designed to have Terri's feeding tube reinserted.

"A woman's life is at stake, and it is absolutely imperative that we take action today."

—SENATOR KENT CONRAD (R–NORTH DAKOTA)

SUNDAY, MARCH 20

Although Terri has spent two days without nourishment or hydration, her family notices little change in her appearance. Her father takes her pulse and checks her skin for dehydration. He examines her pupils with a key-chain flashlight—until police see the flashlight and tell him he can no longer bring it into the room.

Only a few senators are present in the unprecedented session, held on a rainy afternoon in the middle of the Easter recess. The House debate will follow, as members hastily return from their home districts.

"Right now, murder is being committed against a defenseless American citizen."

—REPRESENTATIVE TOM DELAY (R-TEXAS)

"This is heart-wrenching for all Americans. But the issue before this Congress is not an emotional one. It is simply one that respects the rule of law."

— REPRESENTATIVE ROBERT WEXLER (D-FLORIDA)

MONDAY, MARCH 21

Waiting for Congress to vote on the bill that might save Terri's life, her family spends all night in the thrift store.

After three hours of heated partisan debate, the U.S. House passes, by a 203–58 margin, U.S. Senate Compromise Bill 686 "for the relief of the parents of Theresa Marie Schiavo." The bill would transfer the case to a U.S. District Court for review.

President Bush flies back from his ranch in Crawford, Texas, to sign the bill into law in Washington, D.C.

"It is always wise to err on the side of life."

— PRESIDENT GEORGE W. BUSH

Judge James D. Whittemore, a federal judge randomly selected by a computer program to preside over the hearing mandated by the newly signed federal law, hears two hours of arguments yet refuses to rule immediately on whether the state courts had violated Terri's right to due process and her religious beliefs. The Schindlers argue that Terri was a practicing Roman Catholic and the removal of her feeding tube goes against church teaching.

"We are now in a position where a court has ordered her to disobey her church and even jeopardize her eternal soul," says David Gibbs, lawyer for the Schindler family.

George Felos, Michael Schiavo's attorney, argues that reinserting the feeding tube would "countenance a severe invasion upon the body of Terri Schiavo."

TUESDAY, MARCH 22

After four days being deprived of food and hydration, Terri is described by her father as appearing lethargic and stressed.

"She looks like an Auschwitz survivor," Robert Schindler says. "Her skin is sunken. Her eye sockets are sticking out. Her cheekbones dominate her face. Her teeth are protruding."

George Felos describes Terri as "stable, peaceful and calm."

"This whole 'death with dignity' is nothing but a big lie. I'm a witness to my sister slowly dying by this death by dehydration and starvation, and it's one of the most horrific, barbaric experiences."

—BOBBY SCHINDLER

Judge James Whittemore denies an emergency request by the Schindlers to reinsert Terri's feeding tube. They appeal the decision to the Eleventh Circuit Court.

A year after Pope John Paul II stated the Church's position that "the administration of water and food is not a medical procedure," the Vatican makes a rare official statement on a specific right-to-die case.

"The end of life is a question only in the hands of God. This is our belief. It is not something that must be in the hands of politicians," Cardinal Javier Lozano, the pontiff's council for health, says in a radio broadcast. The pope himself is incapacitated and thought to be near death.

WEDNESDAY, MARCH 23

In a two-to-one vote, the Eleventh Circuit Court denies the Schindlers' appeal. The Schindlers file another emergency petition with U.S. Supreme Court.

Florida governor Jeb Bush succeeds in getting a state court to hear new motions in the case, based upon an affidavit by a neurologist who argues that Terri Schiavo is not in a persistent vegetative state. Bush asks the Florida Department of Children and Families to obtain custody of Terri in order to investigate allegations of abuse.

THURSDAY, MARCH 24

The U.S. Supreme Court rejects pleas to intervene in the case.

Judge George Greer issues a restraining order prohibiting the Florida Department of Children and Families from removing Terri Schiavo from the hospice or reinserting the feeding tube. He also denies a petition from the DCF to investigate allegations of abuse and neglect by Michael Schiavo. In addition, Greer rejects an affidavit submitted by the neurologist claiming that Terri Schiavo is not in a persistent vegetative state.

The Florida State Supreme Court rejects the Schindlers' appeal of Greer's rulings. Another hearing before Judge Whittemore lasts four hours without a decision.

A man is arrested after he enters a gun store in Seminole, Florida, and threatens the owner with a box cutter, demanding a weapon so he can rescue Terri Schiavo.

FRIDAY, MARCH 25

After Terri has gone a week without nourishment or hydration, Mary Schindler stops visiting her daughter.

> "It's too painful for me to see her. She had a skeleton look in her face. I couldn't watch my daughter starve to death."
>
> —MARY SCHINDLER

"She appeared very calm. I saw no evidence of bodily discomfort whatever."

—GEORGE FELOS

Judge Whittemore denies another motion by the Schindlers to reinsert the feeding tube. They appeal to the Eleventh Circuit Court of Appeals, which affirms Whittemore's ruling. The Schindlers announce that they will pursue no further federal appeals. They file an emergency motion with Judge Greer, claiming that they heard Terri try to say "I want to live."

Deprived of nourishment and water for almost seven days, Terry begins to show signs of dehydration. Her skin is flaky, her tongue and lips are dry, her eyes are sunken.

George Felos calls for the Schindlers to give up their battle to reinsert Terri's feeding tube. "It's time for that to stop as we approach this Easter weekend and that Mrs. Schiavo be able to die in peace."

SATURDAY, MARCH 26

The Schindlers advise supporters to return home and spend Easter with their families. Many of them remain. In all, fifty-one people are arrested for trying to bring food or water to Terri. Most of them don't get past the first police barricade. When there is an arrest, or some other threat, the area goes into lockdown. Traffic is stopped, Terri's room is secured. There is a SWAT team in place with a sniper on the rooftop.

Following remarks by Operation Rescue founder Terry Randall, members of a group called Revolutionary Communist Youth Brigade seize the microphones and call Terry "a Christian fascist thug."

SUNDAY, MARCH 27

*"Terri is declining rapidly. We believe she has, at this point,
passed where physically she would be able to recover."*
—DAVID GIBBS, LAWYER FOR THE SCHINDLER FAMILY

Terri receives Holy Communion from Monsignor Thaddeus Malanowski and the hospice chaplain. Malanowski gives her a drop of Communion wine on her tongue, but is unable to give her the host because her tongue is too dry and parched.

The Schindlers appeal to Governor Jeb Bush to take Terri into protective custody. Judge Greer has issued a restraining order, which the governor says he must respect.

*"I cannot violate a court order. I don't have power from the U.S.
Constitution, or the Florida Constitution for that matter, that
would allow me to intervene after a decision has been made."*
—GOVERNOR JEB BUSH

MONDAY, MARCH 28

Anticipating Terri's death, CBS News mistakenly posts an already written obituary on their Web site.

*Surrounded by stuffed animals and medical equipment in her
small hospice room in Pinellas Park, Fla., Theresa Marie
Schindler Schiavo died TK.*
—CBS OBITUARY OF TERRI SCHIAVO

After ten days without food or hydration, Terri is still hanging on to life. She has stopped urinating, a sign of kidney failure.

The hospice staff has administered morphine suppositories to Terri twice since the removal of her feeding tube. The Schindlers fear that they are trying to hasten her death.

Michael Schiavo calls a press conference and asks that an autopsy be conducted following his wife's death. Dr. Jon Thogmartin, medical examiner in charge of Pinellas County, issues a press release stating that he will conduct an autopsy because state law requires it, and that "family requests are immaterial."

TUESDAY, MARCH 29

"She is failing, but she is still with us."

— ROBERT SCHINDLER

Terri's heart starts beating rapidly. Her skin is increasingly mottled and her breathing more shallow and difficult. Now she breathes only through her mouth. The flesh inside her mouth and throat has turned a dark red. She is apparently nearing death.

Michael Schiavo's sister Joan tells police that a man drove by her Philadelphia-area home and yelled, "If Terri dies, I'm coming back to shoot you and your family."

Reverend Jesse Jackson arrives at the hospice, calling Terri's situation "an injustice." He asks permission to see Terri and Michael Schiavo does not allow it. Jackson leads a prayer service outside the hospice.

WEDNESDAY, MARCH 30

Terri's skin begins to turn blue. She breathes rapidly. Her eyes are half-open, the pupils moving back and forth very quickly. The veins in her eyelids are red. She is cold and clammy after experiencing a fever the night before.

"If you could say what death looks like, that's how she looks."
—SUZANNE VITADAMO

The Schindlers exhaust their final legal options when the Eleventh U.S. Circuit Court denies their motion for rehearing and the U.S. Supreme Court denies the hearing of an emergency appeal of that ruling.

THURSDAY, MARCH 31

Bobby Schindler and Suzanne Vitadamo have been in Terri's room for an hour and forty-five minutes, praying with a family priest, when a nurse comes in. The nurse takes Terri's pulse and quickly leaves the room. Down the hall, a hospice administrator informs Michael Schiavo that his wife is approaching death. A police officer tells Bobby and Suzanne they will have to leave.

Bobby gets into an argument with the police officer. They go out and call their attorney. He phones back after a couple minutes to tell them he has just received a phone call from Michael Schiavo's attorney, to tell them that Terri died just a few minutes after Suzanne and Bobby were kicked out of her room.

When Terri Schiavo dies at 9:05 A.M., present are Michael Schiavo, his brother Brian, his attorneys, George Felos and Deborah Bushnell, and hospice workers.

When Mary Schindler sees her daughter for the first time in a week, she breaks down sobbing and throws herself on top of her. The police refuse to let Terri's uncle in the room because he isn't immediate family. The Schindlers ask the police to leave the room so they can spend some time alone with their daughter. Their request is refused.

> *"Mrs. Schiavo died a calm, peaceful and gentle death. . . . She had a right to have her last and final moments on this earth to be experienced by a spirit of love and not acrimony. I emphasize it because this death was not for the siblings and not for the spouse and not for the parents. This was for Terri."*
>
> — GEORGE FELOS

> *"May God give grace to our families. After these recent years of neglect at the hands of those who were supposed to protect and care for her, she is finally at peace with God for eternity."*
>
> — SUZANNE VITADAMO

Terri's body is taken to Pinellas County Coroner's Office for an autopsy by district medical examiner Jon R. Thogmartin. Following the autopsy, Terri Schiavo's body will be taken to Pennsylvania and cremated, with the ashes buried in an undisclosed location. Michael Schiavo refused to let the Schindler family come to the funeral and to date, will not tell them where Terri's remains are buried, despite the fact that a court order required him to do so. Michael Schiavo's brother said in a television interview that despite the court order, he wasn't going to tell the Schindlers anything until he decides what to do with Terri's remains.

TERRI SCHIAVO IS DEAD. Whether or not this was her wish, whether or not removing her feeding tube was the right thing to do, her life, and the public drama surrounding it, is over. Some people vow to fight on, while others try to put it behind them. Yet throughout all the complex legal proceedings and highly charged debates, very few people were asking the most important question: How did Terri Schiavo end up with severe brain damage in the first place?

Despite all the attention her death has generated, nobody seems to know exactly what happened to Terri Schiavo in the early morning hours of February 25, 1990. Some claim it was cardiac arrest brought on by a potassium imbalance that resulted from bulimia. Others suggest she was assaulted by Michael Schiavo. Where is the truth?

However you feel about euthanasia or the right to life, if Terri's initial injury was caused by violence or neglect, her death is now a homicide. And there are no statutes of limitation for that crime.

CHAPTER TWO

"Something's Wrong with Terri"

Terri Schiavo was born on December 3, 1963. She grew up in Huntington Park, Pennsylvania, a suburb of Philadelphia. She was the oldest of three children born to Robert and Mary Schindler. Brother Bobby was a year younger and sister Suzanne three years her junior. Robert Schindler owned a heavy-equipment business, and the family was comfortably middle-class.

Family and childhood friends remember Terri as being shy, even timid, around people she didn't know, but very warm and outgoing among those to whom she was close.

"Terri was a very loving, carefree person," childhood friend Sue Cobb Pickwell told me. "She had a very happy demeanor. She always made you laugh."

Terri loved animals, keeping rabbits, gerbils, hamsters, turtles, and tropical fish until she got her beloved Labrador retriever, Bucky. While untrained as an artist, she had a natural talent for drawing. She was raised Catholic, attended parochial school from grades one through twelve, and went to mass every Sunday with her family.

"It was a typical family. Very close," Bobby Schindler said. "We spent a lot of time together."

Overweight as a teenager, Terri weighed as much as two hundred pounds. After graduating from Archbishop Wood High School in Warminster Township in 1981, Terri went on the Nutri-System diet program—a supervised and nutritionally balanced eating plan—losing sixty pounds in a little more than a year.

The weight loss changed her life.

"Terri was always a quietly happy person, until she got thin," her mother told me. "Then she came out of her shell."

"When she lost that weight, she just bloomed," her sister, Suzanne Vitadamo, remembers. "The Terri that had been inside her came out."

In 1982, Terri started attending classes at Bucks County Community College and met Michael Schiavo in a sociology class. He was the first boy she ever dated.

Diane Meyer, friends with Terri since they were two years old, remembers that Terri was so excited about the date that she wanted her to come down from college for the weekend to help her prepare.

On their second date, Michael gave Terri a single red rose and said he wanted to marry her. That night, Terri took Michael to introduce him to Sue Cobb Pickwell and her sister. Terri told them Michael wanted to marry her.

"What, are you crazy?" Sue remembers saying. "It's only your second date. Give it time. Get to know somebody first."

Michael came from a blue-collar family, the youngest of five boys. While some of Terri's friends and family were skeptical about how quick the relationship was progressing, they were happy to see her with someone.

"She fell quickly and hard," Diane remembers. "And when Michael met Terri, she was beautiful."

Terri was driving a T-bird owned by her father's business. She was feeling very good about herself.

While she never dated before she met Michael, Terri had always dreamed of getting married. She and Diane would go to bridal shops and take turns pretending they were preparing a wedding as they tried on wedding dresses.

It happened for real on November 10, 1984. Terri and Michael were married in a Catholic ceremony. Michael, raised a Lutheran, was given special dispensation.

Just prior to the wedding, Terri had gotten a job as a field-service representative for Prudential. Michael worked as a manager in a Philadelphia McDonald's. They rented a town house, but soon found they couldn't afford it, so they moved into the basement of the Schindlers' home. In 1986, Robert and Mary decided to move to a condo they owned in St. Petersburg, Florida. Terri asked if she and Michael could move there and live with them until her husband found a job. Her parents agreed, and the young couple relocated to Florida before Terri's parents.

After living together with Terri and Michael for several months, Robert and Mary bought a house and let the young couple stay in the condo. In 1988, Terri and Michael got their own apartment in North St. Petersburg, about twenty minutes away from her parents' house. Terri had gotten a transfer from her job at Prudential. Michael had sporadic employment prior to finding a job at Agostino's, an upscale Italian restaurant, where he worked as a manager. Terri worked Monday through Friday, from 7:30 A.M. until 3:15 P.M. Michael worked nights.

FEBRUARY 24, 1990

There are conflicting stories throughout this case, so we might as well begin with one of the more troubling instances. Michael has testified that he didn't see Terri the morning of February 24, 1990. His testimony is vague as to whether he saw her later that day. He has said in statements to the police that they hadn't had "any major arguments" that day. Because they worked different hours, Terri and Michael would usually see each other on Saturdays, before Michael went to work, and all day Sunday.

Jackie Rhodes, a friend of Terri's from Prudential, spoke to her on the telephone that afternoon.

> *"It had been a big joke that week at work because she was going for a hair appointment on Saturday and she had dyed her hair blond. . . . She had to decide whether or not she wanted to stay a blond or if she was going back to her natural color. So I called her Saturday afternoon and asked her, well, are you a blonde or a brunette? She said I'm still a blonde. But she was very, very upset when I was talking to her. It sounded like she had been crying. I asked her if she was okay. She said she had a fight with Michael. That he was extremely upset with her because she had spent, I think she told me $80, on her hair that day to stay blonde."*
> —JACKIE RHODES, TESTIMONY, JANUARY 26, 2000,
> GUARDIANSHIP TRIAL

When I spoke with her, Jackie told me that Terri was unhappy in her marriage and was thinking about getting a divorce. At the time, Jackie herself was in counseling for her marriage, and she eventually did divorce. The two girls talked about leaving their husbands and getting an apartment together. They had even gone shopping for furniture at JCPenney.

> *"Our relationship was great. . . . We never discussed divorce. There was no need to discuss it."*
> —MICHAEL SCHIAVO, DEPOSITION, NOVEMBER 19, 1993

Jackie doesn't know if Terri ever mentioned divorce to Michael, but she remains certain they did have a fight that day.

"She was contemplating getting her natural color because it was less expensive," Jackie told me. "Michael wanted her to go back to the brown, probably because she was getting too much attention as a blonde."

When she called that afternoon, Jackie asked if Terri wanted her to come over. Terri said that she had already made plans to go see her brother, Bobby, who lived in the same apartment complex. "She didn't seem like her normal, jovial self," Jackie says. "Her voice was funny. She just didn't sound good."

When Terri came over to Bobby's apartment, she was upset. She told him she and Michael had been fighting, but she didn't go into details. A few weeks earlier, Terri had taken Bobby aside during a dinner at Bennigan's and told him she couldn't stand being married to Michael and wished she had the guts to ask for a divorce. Bobby asked her if she wanted to go out with him and his roommate that night. Terri told Bobby she couldn't. She ironed the jeans he was planning to wear and invited them over for dinner the following night.

Terri attended afternoon mass with her parents at St. John's Church in St. Petersburg Beach. The mass began around 5:00 P.M. and lasted an hour. Immediately after the service, Terri and her parents went to dinner at the house of a friend, Fran Cassler.

Dinner was prepared by a friend of Fran's who was an Italian chef. They all ate a lot, Terri no more than anyone else. Nobody remembers her spending a long time in the bathroom or anything else that might indicate she had purged after the meal. The others drank wine, but Terri didn't.

Her only physical complaint that night was a nagging yeast infection. After dinner, Mary Schindler suggested that Terri come back with her and her husband.

Terri drove her car to her parents' house and spent a half hour visiting with them. She didn't like driving at night and wanted to be home when Michael got off work later. She left her parents' house around 8:00 P.M. Mary told her to buy some medication for

her infection on the way and to call once she got home. She promised that Monday morning she would take her daughter to find a
new gynecologist. Terri was seeing a gynecologist through her Prudential health-care plan. She had been prescribed progesterone to
bring on her period because her menstrual cycles had been slight
and irregular.

When Terri got back to Thunder Bay Apartments, she went to
see Bobby, who was about to leave with his roommate. He asked
her once again if she wanted to go out with them, and Terri said
no. She went back to her place and at approximately eight-thirty
called her mother. Terri told her that she had bought the medication, but not applied it yet. During the phone call, Terri cried,
complaining about the discomfort. She didn't say anything about
her argument with Michael earlier that day, nor did she talk about
getting a divorce.

"Put the stuff on and go to bed," Mary told her daughter just before hanging up. "Monday we'll go see a doctor."

FEBRUARY 25, 1990

Some time early the next morning, the phone rang at the
Schindler home. Robert answered, concerned that there might be
an emergency.

"Terri has passed out and I can't wake her up," Michael said. He
sounded worried and nervous.

"Hang up and call 911 right now," Robert said, then immediately called Bobby at home.

"Something's wrong with Terri," he told Bobby. "Go over there
and see what's going on."

Bobby got dressed and ran over to Terri's apartment. Michael
opened the door for him. While Bobby went in to see Terri,
Michael stayed in the living room, sitting on the sofa and wringing
his hands. He was very nervous and upset.

"I don't know what happened," Michael kept saying.

The lights were on in the living room, kitchen, hallway, and bathroom. From the doorway Bobby could see his sister Terri lying on the floor in the hall near the bathroom. She was facedown, her right cheek against the floor. Her hands were clenched against her chest just beneath her neck.

Bobby touched her shoulder.

"Terri? Terri?"

She made gurgling noises, like a loud snore. Hearing his sister breathe, Bobby figured that whatever happened wasn't serious. Maybe she had just passed out. Bobby didn't have much time to do anything other than shake her shoulder and call her name because shortly after he arrived, the paramedics showed up. Bobby got out of the way and let them take over.

At 5:52 A.M. paramedics from the St. Petersburg Fire Department and SunStar Medic One ambulance service responded to a medical emergency call at 12201 Ninth Street North, St. Petersburg, apartment 2210. The male resident husband had called 911 after having discovered his wife unconscious and unresponsive on the floor in their apartment.

Upon arrival, the paramedics turned Terri over on her back and moved her into the hallway. They found no heartbeat, respiration, or blood pressure. Over the next forty-two minutes, they tried desperately to resuscitate the victim. The paramedics performed CPR, administered multiple doses of epinephrine, as well as lidocaine and Narcan. They defibrillated her seven times.

"I'd be surprised if she makes it to the hospital," Bobby heard one of the paramedics say.

Meanwhile, the firemen called for assistance from the local police.

"They found a subject in question [Theresa] lying face down and unconscious halfway in and halfway out of a bathroom. . . . She

showed no outward signs of violence. The police were called
because of her age and because the situation seemed unusual."

— POLICE REPORT

Before the police came, the firemen questioned Bobby about possible drug use.

"They didn't seem to believe that Terri wasn't on drugs," Bobby told me. "They were almost threatening me, saying 'If she is suffering a drug overdose and you don't tell us, you'll be in a lot of trouble.'"

When a young, apparently healthy female collapses early on a Sunday morning and there are no signs of violence, it's a pretty good assumption that drugs are involved. At the very least, that possibility must be eliminated. There would be a drug screen at the hospital, but the paramedics wanted to know right away, for obvious medical reasons.

It took Bobby some effort to convince them that his sister didn't take drugs or drink to excess. There were also questions concerning AIDS and other sexually transmitted diseases. Obviously, the paramedics were trying to explain why Terri was almost dead.

St. Petersburg police officers Phillip Brewer and Rodney Tower arrived at the scene at 6:33. By then, the paramedics were ready to transport Terri to the hospital. They were still performing CPR as they brought her down the stairs to the ambulance.

"There were no signs of a struggle or anything that would indicate
a crime had been committed. . . . No signs of trauma to her head
and face."

— POLICE REPORT

Moments after the police arrived, Terri was taken away in the ambulance. Bobby called his father and told him Terri was going to Humana Hospital Northside. The police had the keys to Michael and Terri's apartment. They locked up the apartment and then proceeded to the hospital to continue their investigation. Michael rode with Terri in the ambulance. Bobby drove there in his car.

The ambulance arrived at the Humana emergency room at 6:46 A.M. When Terri was brought into the facility, her heart had stopped beating again. ER doctors gave her more Narcan and were able to get her heart beating again. Terri was exhibiting a rapid, fluttering heartbeat and low blood pressure. The doctors found that she had suffered a lack of oxygen to the brain and cardiorespiratory arrest. They could not immediately determine what had caused these two bodily insults.

Terri's blood test showed a potassium deficiency, hypoglycemia, and a low albumin, or protein, level. A drug screen was negative and her blood alcohol rate showed that she had not been drinking.

Robert and Mary Schindler arrived at the hospital around 7:00 A.M. Hospital staffers told them their daughter was in one of the emergency rooms and they couldn't see her. Terri was unconscious, they said, and they were having trouble bringing her back.

Suzanne Schindler Vitadamo was away at school in Orlando. Her mother called her around six-thirty in the morning.

"Something's wrong with Terri," Mary said calmly. "You should come here."

Suzanne got in her car and drove down to St. Petersburg. When she arrived at the emergency room approximately two hours later, she immediately knew that her sister's condition was very serious.

"My parents looked like they had seen a ghost," Suzanne remembers. Her sister was fighting for her life. "I was shocked. I never knew anything to be wrong with Terri."

Meeting the rest of the family in the ICU waiting room, Suzanne hugged everyone. Michael was pacing and very nervous. At the hospital, police interviewed him.

*"[Michael] stated he was awakened this morning when he heard a
thud. He thought his wife had fallen down and got up to check
on her. He found her unconscious on the floor and called the
paramedics. Michael stated he doesn't know what could be wrong
with Theresa. There haven't been any problems at home which
would lead to her wanting to try suicide and they have had no
major arguments lately. . . . She has had recent 'female problems'
and is seeing her gynecologist on a regular basis. She has been
tired lately and not feeling well."*

—POLICE REPORT

A police officer asked Robert Schindler if he thought Michael
could have had anything to do with Terri's condition.

"No. No way," Robert said. When I asked him if, at that time,
he ever suspected Michael of abusing Terri, Robert replied: "I
never went there."

The officers were interested in domestic violence and drugs as
possible explanations for Terri's collapse. They did not speak to
Bobby Schindler, and his name does not appear on the police report. They also did not speak with the victim's mother.

*"A drug screen revealed no amounts of illegal narcotics present
in her system and her blood alcohol level measured at 'less than
10' which a nurse described as being the bottom of the scale."*

—POLICE REPORT

The police waited at the hospital until 8:55 A.M., when they
were told of the results of a CAT scan, which revealed no "midline
shift" of the brain, indicating there was no obvious abnormality
that might have been caused by violent trauma. With those results
and the blood tests showing no drugs or alcohol, it appeared that
Terri's collapse had been caused by some medical condition or accident. If the victim recovered, she would tell doctors what she re-

membered. The case would be routinely sent to homicide in case she died at the hospital.

The police officers had locked up Terri's apartment and returned the keys to Michael without photographing the scene or noting possible evidence for a follow-up investigation. Officer Brewer gave Michael Schiavo a business card and told him he would call for an update of Terri's condition.

"No further action was taken."

— POLICE REPORT

Over the next week, Michael and the rest of the family stayed in the ICU waiting room, sometimes spending the night sleeping in the chairs. Michael's mother and father came down from Pennsylvania. Every time there was a Code Blue, the family thought it was Terri and ran for the door. In fact, she had coded several times while in the ICU, but each time the doctors had been able to bring her back.

"The doctors kept saying, the next twenty-four hours is crucial," Suzanne remembers. "Then the next twenty-four. And the next."

*"The patient remained significantly unstable in the first few days
and did not respond to any kind of stimulation."*

— HUMANA HOSPITAL DISCHARGE SUMMARY

At one point Robert and Suzanne went to the chapel to pray. They were prepared to hear that Terri had died.

"Don't worry," Robert told his daughter, "if they can keep her alive, we'll be able to fix her."

For three days, Terri had been clinging to life. She was given a permanent tracheostomy and kept on a ventilator. She was having uncontrollable seizures, so the doctors gave her phenobarbital. Electroencephalograms (EEGs) and CAT scans were repeated several times to determine the extent of her brain damage. She required blood transfusions. She was being fed through a tube. Shortly after admission, she developed a staph infection and pneumonia.

The family would go in and see her regularly, even though visitors were not normally allowed in ICU rooms.

"There were tubes sticking out of her everywhere," Suzanne remembers. The doctors told Terri's family that she had suffered extensive brain damage. It was too early to tell even whether or not she would survive, much less know what her condition would be if she lived.

Terri's brain had been deprived of oxygen for a significant period of time. She remained unresponsive, but showed some improvement. Her condition eventually stabilized and she was put into her own room. She was taken off the ventilator.

None of the doctors could figure out exactly what had happened to Terri. The morning of her admission to the hospital, they began asking questions about her medical history and personal habits to determine the cause of her collapse.

Various possibilities were considered and dismissed. Terri had no history of strokes, seizures, hypertension, diabetes, or heart disease. She hadn't been taking drugs or drinking. She didn't smoke. She wasn't suffering from an allergic reaction. Other than the yeast infection, she had not shown any recent signs of sickness or distress. Because of the infection, toxic shock syndrome was considered as a possible cause, but eliminated after further testing.

Terri's heart was in pretty good shape, considering it had stopped beating several times. She had not suffered a heart attack, and other than minor problems with heart rate and ejection fraction, her heart was close to normal.

The only abnormalities discovered in her blood work were a potassium deficiency, hypoglycemia, and a low protein level. The first day, she was on a potassium IV, which had pushed her level of potassium up close to normal within twenty-four hours. The doctors speculated that the low potassium level might have provoked cardiac arrest. She had no history of adrenal disease, which might have affected her potassium level. It was very rare to see this, especially in an otherwise healthy young woman, but the doctors could find no other explanation for her collapse, cardiac arrest, and oxygen deprivation. Low potassium can be the result of prolonged and excessive vomiting, diarrhea, or the abuse of diuretics. Bulimics sometimes purge themselves into a state of potassium deficiency by these means.

The attending physician, Dr. Samir Shah, asked the family if Terri drank a lot of coffee. They told him she drank about ten to fifteen glasses of iced tea a day.

"The fact that she drank a lot of iced tea was the only thing we could identify," Mary recalls. "We didn't remember her eating habits being abnormal and never had any suspicions that she had an eating disorder."

At one point, in front of other family members, Michael Schiavo was asked whether his wife threw up after meals. He said no. From other conversations with Michael, Dr. Shah made the following notes.

> "According to her family her diet has been very erratic. She does not eat properly. [Her husband] has to sometimes fight with her to eat a good meal. She has lost 65 lbs. a few years ago. He states that since then she has been tired from time to time. She is weight conscious and there is no history suggestive [of] any problems between the family members or any history of depression, etc. to suggest suicide attempt. There was no seizure activity noted by the husband when he found her."
>
> —HISTORY AND PHYSICAL REPORT, DR. SAMIR SHAH

At the time of her collapse, Terri weighed 126 pounds. She was five feet four and a half inches. Sometimes her weight went up and down within a range of about four pounds, but she didn't have the extreme weight fluctuations associated with bulimia. Nobody remembered her bingeing on food or vomiting after eating. There were no signs that she was using laxatives to purge herself.

All the family could think of was the fact that about seven years earlier she had lost sixty pounds over the period of a year (she dropped another fifteen to twenty pounds over a longer period after marrying Michael) and that she drank a lot of iced tea. They spoke to Dr. Pothen Jacob, a nutritional specialist, who was leaning toward cardiac arrest triggered by low potassium as the explanation for her condition.

> "The etiology of the patient's unconscious state is not known for sure. However, the patient was found to have a significant hypokalemia with potassium down to 2 mEq on admission and family gives history that is highly consistent with bulimia in the past. Patient never admitted to any diuretic abuse, although [this] is a possibility."
>
> —HUMANA HOSPITAL NUTRITIONAL CONSULTATION
> REPORT, DR. POTHEN JACOB

By the time of Terri's discharge on May 9, 1990, the doctors at Humana Hospital still hadn't determined what had happened. None of the doctors' reports reach any precise conclusions regarding the primary event that caused her cardiac arrest and brain damage. She was still nonresponsive and unable to communicate. A consulting doctor recommended that Terri be transferred to a long-term rehabilitation clinic where intensive therapy could be obtained.

> "We felt that as the patient had shown some improvement during her hospitalization, though she was not following commands, in her physical and mental status some improvement was shown. . . .

The patient stayed in the hospital for a very long period of time with several complications, but she improved slowly and gradually and was in stable condition at the time of transfer to the nursing home."

—HUMANA HOSPITAL DISCHARGE SUMMARY

Terri Schiavo remained in that state for the next fifteen years. The cause of her collapse is still unexplained.

CHAPTER THREE

Cause of Death

If Terri Schiavo had died the day she collapsed, or in the hospital shortly afterward, her body would have been autopsied and
the cause of her death determined. The local medical authority—
in this case the Pinellas-Pasco counties medical examiner—would
have issued a death certificate and identified the cause and manner
of death.

But this didn't happen.

Following her death fifteen years later, an autopsy was conducted by Dr. Jon Thogmartin, medical examiner responsible for
Pinellas County. When this book went to press, the autopsy report
had not been completed. Hopefully, the autopsy results will answer some questions about the nature of Terri's brain damage and
the extent of her incapacity. Thogmartin also wants to determine
the cause of Terri's collapse, but it might be too late to gather any
conclusive evidence. He will address the controversy surrounding
allegations of abuse and neglect, and attempt to determine
whether or not Terri was bulimic.

Just prior to Terri's death, Michael Schiavo held a press conference demanding an autopsy. While family members can request an
autopsy, the final determination belongs to the medical examiner.
Because of the controversy over Terri Schiavo's condition and

eventual death, Thogmartin planned to perform an autopsy whether or not Michael Schiavo or the Schindlers asked for one.

In general, autopsies are performed in approximately 25 percent of deaths reported to the medical examiner. A medical examiner makes determinations in four separate categories concerning a death.

Contributing cause of death. This would be a preexisting illness or medical condition that eventually led to the subject's death.

Mechanism of death. This is the medical explanation for death. It is usually highly technical, as in: "Cardiac arrest as a result of cessation of brain function," in a case where someone is shot in the head.

Immediate cause of death. This is the bodily insult, whether trauma, injury, illness, or organ failure, that is the direct cause of the subject's death.

Manner of death. This is how the death is classified, according to the NASH system. Possible manners of death are: Natural, Accidental, Suicide, or Homicide. The medical examiner can also classify a death as unknown. This happens even in cases that are clearly homicides. For example, Laci Peterson was classified an unknown because the medical examiner could not determine exactly how she died.

Many people are under the assumption that a medical examiner conducts autopsies only on persons who are the victim of a homicide. This is a misconception created by the portrayal of medical examiners in movies and television. In real life, as opposed to Hollywood, the cause in any unexplained, undocumented, unsupervised, or accidental death needs to be investigated so the state can issue a death certificate.

In certain circumstances, an accidental death can be effectively investigated by a detective who collects enough evidence, whether testimonial or physical, to determine the immediate cause and manner of death to the satisfaction of the medical examiner, who then decides an autopsy is not necessary. We read about these deaths in the newspaper every day: drownings, car accidents, industrial accidents, etc.

The death of an elderly person under the care of a doctor is most often not a medical examiner's case, and there is no autopsy if an attending physician is willing to sign a death certificate that the death occurred because of natural causes. This is commonly referred to as a "natural" because the deceased died as a result of an illness or disease that was known to their physician, or sometimes simply of old age. More than 90 percent of deaths in this country are due to natural causes. In most of those cases, a doctor can issue a death certificate saying the victim died of natural causes. However, sometimes the circumstances warrant an autopsy to further determine the precise cause of death and whether it might be suspicious.

In deaths that appear to be suicides, there is almost always an autopsy and police investigation. A true suicide is, in fact, a homicide in which the victim and the suspect are the same person. But it is common to find staged suicides, in which a suspect has attempted to make a victim's death appear to be self-inflicted. That is why autopsies are usually conducted in apparent suicides.

An autopsy is a legal and medical procedure. There are two different systems—medical examiner and coroner. Most jurisdictions have one or the other. A coroner does not have to be a forensic pathologist or even a medical doctor. He is an elected law enforcement official with broad powers (sometimes he is the most powerful law enforcement official in his jurisdiction). Coroners might not per-

form the autopsy themselves, but they can ask a forensic pathologist to conduct one. They also have the power to conduct a coroner's inquest. These involve, in effect, grand juries convened to
investigate suspicious deaths. The coroner can subpoena witnesses,
order the release of documents, and conduct investigations.

The medical examiner in Pinellas-Pasco counties does not have
the power to conduct an inquest. If Thogmartin finds anything
suspicious in the autopsy, he will have to request the relevant law
enforcement authority, in this case, the Pinellas county sheriff or
St. Petersburg police, to conduct a further investigation.

When an autopsy uncovers important evidence for use in a
homicide investigation, it's not the medical examiner's responsibility to identify a suspect or build a case against him for criminal
prosecution. This is the job of a homicide detective. Even in cases
that do not lead to criminal prosecution, the forensic pathologist
needs detectives, who can look at the circumstances surrounding
the victim's body and help him make determinations. Some medical examiners, like those in Pinellas-Pasco counties, have investigators who work for the medical examiner, but they are not
charged with solving the case, only with collecting more information so that the M.E. can make his own conclusions regarding the
causes, mechanism, and manner of death.

The medical examiner's expertise is focused on the best evidence of the case—the victim's body. Yet there is other evidence,
and it's up to the homicide detective to gather, analyze, and explain it. The homicide detective must be able to understand the
forensic evidence provided by the medicolegal examination of the
victim's body, but his investigation also considers other realms of
evidence. He examines the social context of the crime—the victim's lifestyle and personality, family and friends, any problems he
might be having in his personal and professional life—in order to
see who might possibly have been involved in his death.

In any obvious homicide, there is always an autopsy. This procedure is ordered not necessarily to establish who committed the murder, but to determine the cause and manner of death. When you see a victim lying on the ground with a knife protruding from his chest, you might think the autopsy is just a formality. But when, for example, the forensic pathologist finds multiple gunshot wounds inflicted prior to the knife wound, everything is changed.

Sometimes the medical examiner's determination might appear obvious as a result of the observable cause of death, yet the toxicology reports shows otherwise—for example, when it is discovered that a lethal poison in the bloodstream caused clinical death before a knife was plunged into a victim's chest. The medical examiner can prove that the secondary injury did not cause death, but could be part of a staged crime scene.

Because he is able to closely examine the best evidence of a possible homicide—the victim's body—with detailed information and expertise, the medical examiner can often see things of which the homicide detective could not have been aware. And there are enough strange circumstances to require a forensic pathologist, whether medical examiner or coroner, to scientifically determine cause and manner of death, no matter how obvious they might appear at the crime scene.

Once an autopsy is conducted, the homicide detective has a determinate source of evidence that can corroborate or contradict other evidence, such as statements by witnesses or the suspect, timeline, and other forensics recovered from the scene. The homicide detective then takes this evidence, considers it all in context, and begins to put together the pieces of the puzzle. If there are enough pieces, he can close the case. Sometimes the evidence is insufficient, and the case stays open. The longer the case stays open, the less likely it is to ever be solved.

Unexplained death is a circumstance that needs to be weighed differently in every case. Some deaths are caused by illnesses that remain undiagnosed until the time of death. Other people die of poisons or infections that are not detected until after their demise. And what if there are no physical symptoms to support the medical hypothesis of death? What if the patient dies without a clear cause of illness or injury? This is exactly where we find ourselves with the Terri Schiavo case.

The autopsy can answer certain questions about the victim's death. And it provides a wealth of evidence useful in determining the cause and manner of death. However, you need a detective to make sense of all the circumstances surrounding the death in order to solve the murder. The forensic pathologist's expertise does not go beyond the victim's body. The detective's case starts at the victim's body, and then radiates out to include everything else.

If Terri Schiavo had died fifteen years ago, and during the subsequent autopsy the medical examiner did not find some preexisting illness or evidence of natural bodily insult, he would have declared her death to be unnatural or possibly a homicide. The case had already been routed to the St. Petersburg homicide detectives in the event Terri died at the hospital. A homicide investigation would have been undertaken, and hopefully some determination made as to whether or not Michael Schiavo had any responsibility for his wife's death, whether intentional or through negligence.

When Terri Schiavo was first seen by the fire-department paramedics who responded to her apartment, they found her lying facedown in the bathroom doorway. She had no pulse, no blood pressure, no respiration. If her heart was still beating, it was just strong enough to keep her brain, heart, and kidneys functional. Seconds earlier, when her brother, Bobby, saw her, Terri was experiencing difficulty with her respiration, which might possibly have been agonal breathing—the final gasps prior to death. Her body was shutting down. She didn't have much time left.

The fire-department paramedics were capable of providing basic life support. They performed CPR—clearing her airway, checking her pulse and respiration—but they didn't have very sophisticated technology or medication. While CPR alone couldn't have saved Terri's life, it would have provided her with much-needed oxygen and helped minimize or stop brain damage.

When the ambulance technicians from SunStar arrived, they took over, being better equipped and more qualified. One of the SunStar paramedics continued CPR while the other began to insert large-bore IV needles for fluids and medication. When they hooked up EKG leads to measure Terri's cardiac rate, they found she didn't have one. They treated her with epinephrine to stimulate the heart. Then they took out the defibrillating paddles and tried to jump-start her heart.

Eventually she would be given lidocaine to suppress ventricular fibrillations (unsynchronized heartbeats with no pumping action) and Narcan, a harmless and fast-acting medication routinely given to patients suffering possible drug overdoses (which the paramedics suspected at one point might have occurred), and epinephrine, a potent agent that jump-starts the heart. Regardless of what occurred at the apartment before the paramedics arrived, or how long it took them to get her heart beating again, Terri Schiavo had been deprived of oxygen for a significant period of time.

Some forty minutes and seven defibrillations later, the paramedics were ready to put Terri in the ambulance and take her to the hospital. The amount of time they spent at the scene indicates that they could not stabilize the patient in order to transport her. They probably had a hard time inserting the IVs—it's not easy to find a vein on someone whose heart isn't beating. And it's clear from the number of defibrillations that her heart was having difficulty beating on its own.

At Humana Hospital, she flatlined again. Once the emergency-room doctors performed lifesaving measures to reestablish a stable heart function, they had to attempt to determine the cause of her cardiorespiratory arrest. Blood tests were taken and analyzed. She was given an electrocardiogram. Her heart showed some sinus tachycardia (increased heartbeat due to irritation of the heart) and reduced ejection fraction. Her enzyme levels did not indicate a myocardial infarction (heart attack), and there was no necrotic tissue noted in the heart muscle.

This brings up an important misunderstanding that appears to have plagued many people who closely followed the Schiavo case, including bloggers, public commentators, and even some medical experts who ought to know better. Terri Schiavo did not suffer a heart attack.

HOW DO WE KNOW IF SOMEONE HAS SUFFERED A HEART ATTACK?

A heart attack occurs when the blood supply to part of the heart muscle itself—the myocardium—is severely reduced or ceases entirely. The medical term for heart attack is *myocardial infarction*.

> *"Myocardial infarction is the death of heart muscle from the sudden blockage of a coronary artery by a blood clot. Blockage of a coronary artery deprives the heart muscle of blood and oxygen causing injury to the heart muscle. If blood flow is not restored within twenty to forty minutes irreversible death of the heart muscle will begin to occur. Muscle continues to die for six to eight hours at which time the heart attack usually is complete. The dead heart muscle is replaced by scar tissue."*
>
> — MEDICINENET.COM

Myocardial infarction usually affects the left ventricle, the chamber of the heart that forces oxygenated blood away from the heart through the arteries to other organs, including the brain. The infarcted muscle undergoes a sequence of changes during the healing process. Initially the infarcted muscle appears bruised and cyanotic as a result of blood stagnation in a portion of the heart.

When a heart attack occurs, cardiac enzymes are released from the cells. These enzymes will be elevated if a heart attack has occurred or is in progress. The release of enzymes follows a characteristic pattern over time shortly after myocardial infarction. Enzyme elevations cannot be the only indicator of myocardial damage. They need to be supported by the electrocardiographic changes in the heart measured by the EKG.

An EKG measures the function of the heart through the display of three waves on a graph, described as "Q" waves, "S-T" segment waves, and "T" waves. During acute myocardial infarction the Q waves are pronounced, the S-T segment waves are elevated, and the T waves are inverted. Over time the S-T and T waves return to normal, but Q waves persist as electrocardiographic evidence of a previous infarction.

This means that no matter when a person has a heart attack, there will always be evidence when a doctor views the EKG. The doctor might not be able to say exactly when that infarction occurred, but he can be certain that it did. The diagnosis is not left up to the physician's opinion because the machine lists the causes of the abnormalities it is recording. The EKG is not a test open to various interpretations.

Terri had both an EKG and enzyme-level testing performed at Humana shortly after being admitted. Both showed negative for heart attack. These notations from Terri Schiavo's medical records at Humana Hospital prove that evidence of a heart attack was not present in her body.

> "Serial EKGs in the first few days did not show any evidence of myocardial infarction. . . .
> "Enzymes did not reveal evidence of myocardial infarction."
> —HUMANA HOSPITAL DISCHARGE SUMMARY,
> MAY 9, 1990

In other words, the medical evidence is clear and irrefutable that Terri Schiavo did not have a heart attack.

She did, however, suffer cardiac arrest.

CARDIAC ARREST

Everybody dies of cardiac arrest. That's when the heart stops beating, for whatever reason. Terri Schiavo suffered cardiac arrest on two separate occasions—when she collapsed on February 25, 1990, and when she died on March 31, 2005. The first event was either cardiac arrest resulting from some other cause or sudden cardiac arrest.

Sudden cardiac arrest is the abrupt loss of cardiac function as a result of an electrical malfunction in the heart. It is not the same thing as a heart attack. The cardiac rhythm is disturbed to the point where the heart either stops beating entirely, or it does not beat strongly enough to maintain the vital organs and keep the body alive. The vast majority of people who suffer sudden cardiac arrest do not get help in time and wind up dying from sudden cardiac death (the term for cardiac arrest resulting in death). Once cardiac arrest has occurred, the patient has only a few minutes to live, unless she is treated.

Most cardiac arrests that result in sudden death are caused by ventricular fibrillation (when the electrical impulses become chaotic), ventricular tachycardia (when the impulses become rapid), or both.

In ventricular fibrillation, cardiac output is impaired because the lower chambers of the heart quiver instead of pumping as a result of abnormal electrical activity. The chambers contract in a rapid and unsynchronized fashion. The heart will pump little or no blood. Ventricular fibrillation is very dangerous, resulting in a cardiac rate as high as 350 beats per minute. The victim will collapse and death will follow within minutes—unless emergency medical care is administered. A defibrillator can shock the heart into regaining its normal rhythm. Ventricular fibrillation is typically found in younger victims of cardiac arrest. There are several different diseases that can lead to cardiac arrest, none of which were indicated in Terri Schiavo's medical records or history. There are also possible genetic or congenital causes that might not have been identified during her hospital care.

Terri Schiavo's heart was fibrillating when the paramedics found her. She was in the state they would call PEA (pulseless electrical activity). This is clear from the kind of treatment she received—lidocaine for fibrillation, and seven separate defibrillations.

Cardiac arrest can occur without warning, yet it rarely strikes unless there are other factors present. Ninety percent of the time, it occurs because of a myocardial infarction caused by narrowed or blocked cardiac arteries. Cardiac arrest can also be caused by bodily insults that are not organic in nature, such as respiratory arrest, choking, drowning, electrocution, and trauma. Sometimes cardiac arrest can occur without any known cause.

Between 1989 and 1996, there was a 32 percent increase of sudden cardiac deaths among young women aged fifteen to thirty-four, according to the Centers for Disease Control. Researchers attribute this dramatic increase to obesity, smoking, and inactivity. Terri Schiavo was not overweight. She did not smoke. While she might not have been athletic, she had an active life.

Brain death begins to occur four to six minutes following cardiac arrest, due to a lack of oxygenated blood to the brain. Death can come shortly afterward. If the victim is treated within minutes of the cardiac arrest, defibrillation can restore the heartbeat.

*"A victim's chances of survival are reduced by 7 to 10 percent
with every minute that passes without defibrillation. Few attempts
at resuscitation succeed after 10 minutes."*

—AMERICAN HEART ASSOCIATION

The fact that Terri Schiavo survived, even if she did suffer serious brain damage, indicates that, if she experienced sudden cardiac arrest, it occurred just prior to or at the time when the paramedics arrived. It is also possible that her heart went into fibrillation more gradually, decreasing the oxygen to her brain over a longer period of time. Bobby clearly heard her breathing, even if it was agonal. Michael's statements are unclear as to whether she was breathing or not.

The paramedics saved Terri's life. Approximately 95 percent of cardiac-arrest victims die before reaching the hospital. The survival rate improves to nearly 50 percent when defibrillation is provided within five to seven minutes. When someone survives cardiac arrest they are said to have an "aborted" sudden cardiac death, because death would have occurred without intervention. They will now have an increased risk of cardiac arrest in the future. After the first couple days in the hospital, Terri did not have any more documented cardiac events. Her EKGs at Humana, taken as early as her day of admission, showed some sinus tachycardia (increased cardiac rate caused by irritation to the heart) and a reduced ejection fraction (35 percent the first day increasing to 65 percent a few days later).

No one determined what caused Terri's cardiac arrest, whether it was the primary bodily insult or the result of some other event. One thing is certain, however: Her heart stopped beating for several minutes, and she hovered on the edge of death for a very long time.

After her collapse, Terri exhibited no further signs of cardiac problems. Her heart remained healthy, even strong. Her feeding tube was removed three times. On the first two occasions, she went two days and six days without food or hydration and did not suffer any cardiac event. The third time her feeding tube was removed, doctors estimated it would take her seven to fourteen days to die. She lasted fourteen days.

As Pat Anderson, an attorney for the Schindler family, points out: "The reason it took Terri so long to die was that her heart was healthy."

CHAPTER FOUR

Bulimia

Cardiac arrest provoked by potassium deprivation as the result of bulimia has been the cause of death most often cited for Terri Schiavo. Yet it remains a hypothesis. Despite the way this cause of death has often been referred to in the media, and even accepted by the courts, it has never been medically proven that Terri was bulimic.

Bulimia, also known as bulimia nervosa, is an eating disorder in which the subject engages in binge eating, followed by purging brought on by induced vomiting, or the abuse of diuretics or laxatives to keep the body from digesting the recently eaten food and therefore not processing the calories. Bulimia is not to be confused with anorexia nervosa, which is simply not eating food.

While some bulimia sufferers are able to hide their illness from friends and family, it creates physical symptoms and behavioral changes that can be seen, at least in retrospect. The damage to the body is gradual, yet dramatic, and the longer the subject suffers from the illness, the worse these manifestations are.

Physical Effects

Frequent weight changes. Weight can fluctuate between periods of binging and purging.

Vomiting. Frequent and long periods of vomiting.

Tooth decay from gastric acids during vomiting. This effect will remain visible long after the subject ceases bulimic behavior.

Swollen salivary glands.

Poor skin and hair loss.

Irregular periods.

Loss of interest in sex.

Lethargy and tiredness.

Increased risk of heart problems.

Psychological Symptoms

Uncontrollable urges to eat vast amounts of food.

An obsession with food.

Distorted perception of body weight and shape.

Mood swings.

Anxiety and depression.

Isolation.

Behavioral Symptoms

Disappearing to the toilet after meals.

Excessive use of laxatives or diuretics.

Periods of fasting.

Excessive exercise.

Secrecy and reluctance to socialize.

Food disappearing.

Of these above symptoms, only two apply to Terri Schiavo that wouldn't apply to almost every other twenty-six-year-old American female. She had irregular periods and she drank a lot of iced tea, which is a diuretic. Mary Schindler told me that her daughter always had trouble with her periods, even when she was heavier, so that symptom might not have anything to do with her eating habits.

There has been so much written about Terri's medical condition, and we have seen so much video footage of her after the brain damage occurred, that it's easy to forget that this young woman seemed healthy until February 25, 1990. Her only medical complaints were irregular or weak menstruation and a yeast infection. Michael told police the morning of her collapse that Terri had been "tired lately and not feeling well."

Terri had been overweight as a teenager, weighing as much as two hundred pounds. She lost this weight through NutriSystem, a supervised program in which one buys prepared foods and follows a nutritionally balanced diet. In a little more than a year, she lost sixty pounds and never gained the weight back. When she married Michael Schiavo, she weighed approximately one hundred and forty pounds. Over the following three years she lost another fifteen to twenty pounds.

In the beginning hours at Humana Hospital, doctors struggled to determine what had happened to make Terri, an apparently healthy twenty-six-year-old woman, fall into a coma and almost die. Test after test failed to give a complete answer for her condition. She had apparently suffered no recent trauma. She had no previous medical condition. Three things stuck out in her blood work: a potassium deficiency, low protein level, and hypoglycemia. The potassium deficiency was especially troubling, since that can cause cardiac arrest. Taken together, the blood tests seemed to indicate a young woman who had either lost a lot of fluids through diarrhea or diuretics abuse, and might even have had an eating disorder.

Interviews with her family members established that Terri had been overweight as a teenager, and the Humana doctors, particularly Dr. Pothen Jacob, a nutritionist, began speculating that Terri might have been bulimic.

At this point, Terri's family did not know whether or not she would survive. They answered the doctor's questions as thoroughly as possible, hoping that their responses might solve the mystery of Terri's collapse and perhaps even help her condition. The family had also been asked about drugs, alcohol, toxic shock syndrome, and various other possible causes for her collapse. They had been asked if she was depressive or suicidal.

The weight loss and iced-tea drinking were the only abnormalities the Humana doctors could find in her medical history.

> *"Her husband and family indicated that she has been having dizzy spells this week. Her diet is apparently erratic. Several years ago she lost 80 pounds, and she frequently skips breakfast and lunch. To the family's knowledge she does not engage in surreptitious diuretic use or in binge purging."*
>
> —DR. DAVID KOHL, CONSULTING REPORT,
>
> FEBRUARY 25, 1990

Was Terri Schiavo bulimic?

Terri was five feet four and a half inches tall. In the year leading up to her collapse, she weighed between 120 and 123.5 pounds, according to the records of her general practitioner, who saw her four times a year and weighed her at every visit. Going even further back, to that doctor's records in 1987, we see no indication of weight fluctuation greater than four or five pounds.

In all the photos I have seen of Terri after her weight loss, she looks healthy and well nourished, atlhough in some photos she does appear to be very thin. She never exhibited any of the physical manifestations of bulimia or anorexia. By all accounts, Terri was not athletic. She went to the pool, but she did not work out or engage in any strenuous exercise. The way she kept her weight down was by dieting. The question is: Did her diet become a disorder?

Mary Schindler never noticed her daughter going to the bathroom after eating. She never noticed that her daughter was eating excessively or throwing up, or that her weight was fluctuating.

"Our whole family couldn't believe the bulimic thing," Mary says now. I have asked her repeatedly about Terri's eating habits and whether she ever exhibited any of the specific symptoms of bulimia. Mary claims never to have noticed anything out of the ordinary.

Some of Terri's friends offered conflicting views of her eating habits. Diane Meyer, who knew Terri when she was overweight, remembers visiting at Terri and Michael's town house in Pennsylvania shortly after their marriage, when Michael was in McDonald's management training. She remembers Terri cutting a bagel into several pieces and eating only one piece with a small dollop of cream cheese for lunch. Diane grew concerned that Terri wasn't eating enough. It took a lot of effort for Diane to convince Terri to go to a Chinese restaurant, where they had a full meal. When Michael returned, Diane told him, "You've got to do something. Terri's not eating right."

"Mind your own goddamn business," Michael replied.

Marianne Nicholson worked at Prudential. She remembers going out to lunch with Terri almost every day and doesn't recall her having any strange eating habits.

When Jackie Rhodes started working at Prudential, she remembers people at the office teasing Terri about not eating at work. Once they became friends, Jackie and Terri often went out to eat, either alone or with the other girls from the office. Terri introduced Jackie to shellfish—oysters, clams, and mussels. "She had a wide variety of foods that she liked," Jackie recalls, but doesn't remember Terri bingeing, or eating to excess. Terri always carried a small pouch with her to the bathroom, which contained toothpaste, a toothbrush, and mouthwash, and brushed her teeth after a meal.

Some have seen this as symptom of bulimia. Jackie thinks that Terri was proud of her perfect teeth and beautiful smile.

Terri Welch, another colleague at Prudential, seems to think

Terri might have been bulimic, but she doesn't remember anything suspicious except for the trips to the bathroom with her pouch after the other girls had already left. Welch remembers that when they ate at a Wendy's, Terri would go to the salad bar and fill up a big plate of just salad.

Bulimics eat uncontrollably. A big plate of salad might not be very healthy, but it's not the kind of meal you need to purge afterward.

MEDICAL MALPRACTICE

One problem with determining whether or not Terri had bulimia is that a jury trial has found that she did.

Michael Schiavo initiated the malpractice suit, but Robert Schindler was also involved, meeting regularly with plaintiffs' attorney Glenn Woodworth. After researching the case, Woodworth told them that there were no grounds for a malpractice lawsuit. But he obviously hadn't considered bulimia.

"Something happened that's wrong," Robert Schindler said, "and I think you should take a hard look before you throw in the towel."

Woodworth said he would call Gary Fox, a plaintiffs' attorney in Miami. Fox thought there was a viable claim for malpractice based on Terri's doctors' failure to diagnose bulimia.

There was a little problem with this strategy. Terri's bulimia had not been medically established. No one in the family was convinced she was bulimic. While they had speculated about it during conversations with doctors, no one ever came to any conclusions.

Robert supported Fox's strategy, and Michael was also on board. The attorneys would argue that Terri's doctors should have diagnosed her bulimia.

In the trial, held in early November 1992, Terri's husband and immediate family testified that they had no indication she might have been bulimic. Meanwhile, other witnesses offered circumstantial evidence that the plaintiffs' attorneys were able to weave into a narrative describing a girl who had a secret eating disorder—so secret, in fact, that she kept it from everyone close to her.

The medical malpractice case was based on the failure of Terri's gynecologist to diagnose her alleged bulimia (At the request of his insurance company, Terri's general practitioner settled out of court for a reported quarter million dollars without any liability). She had been seeing a gynecologist, a Dr. Igel, because of weak and irregular menstruation. While Terri was the named plaintiff, Michael, as her husband and legal guardian, was also suing for lack of consortium. Loss of consortium is the damages sought by the spouse of an injured party for loss of services, comfort, and conjugal relations as a result of the spouse's injury.

Suzanne Vitadamo told me, "Bulimia is very hard to prove. They sued the doctors for not finding it. Well, the doctors didn't find it, because it wasn't there." This is a question that was relevant then, and is relevant now: Was Terri Schiavo bulimic?

Testifying at the medical malpractice trial, Dr. Minquan Suksanong, an infectious disease specialist at Humana Hospital, was asked if he had formulated an opinion as to the cause of the low-potassium and low-protein readings in Terri's blood tests. He replied: "Apparently she has problem with her eating disorder and may have had nutritional deficiency which may have contributed. . . ."

Q. What caused her heart to stop based upon the evidence that was available to you, in your opinion?

A. I don't think anybody really can, you know, really tell definitely what cause[d] . . . her heart to stop, but the low potassium may have . . . been a contributing factor.

Speaking to Michael Schiavo at the hospital three days after Terri's collapse, Dr. Suksanong learned that Terri had had poor eating habits and had frequent urination after drinking iced tea.

Under redirect questioning, Glenn Woodworth, attorney for the plaintiff, asked Dr. Suksanong:

Q. Tell the jury if it's a fact, if you will, that ultimately it was the consensus of all the physicians who worked on her from February to May at Humana Northside that this young lady collapsed because she wasn't eating right?

A. Correct.

This is clearly an oversimplification of Dr. Suksanong's prior statement. And it doesn't mean the doctors thought Terri was bulimic. It might have been a case of malnutrition due to dieting. Dr. David Baras, a physical-medicine and rehabilitation specialist, was the next to testify.

Q. Were you able to formulate, based on all the information available to you, any reasons for her anoxic encephalopathy?

A. From the information that I gathered, also with the family and her medical records, it appeared to me that she had a cardiac arrest which subsequently caused anoxic encephalopathy which presented herself in a coma to me.

Q. Was there . . . any information available to you as to the cause or the reason for her heart stopping?

A. Yes.

Q. And what was that, sir?

A. There were reports that she had a history of eating disorder and that at the time of admission her potassium and protein from her blood tests were extremely low and this potentially was the cause of her cardiac arrest.

Q. A conclusion was drawn that she had an eating disorder because of something about the way she ate?

A. That's correct.

Once again, a trial lawyer pushes a witness from possibility to certainty—but that's not the point. After my study of all the available medical and legal records, this is the closest thing I can find to a medical opinion by someone who actually treated Terri Schiavo that she suffered cardiac arrest as a result of low potassium level caused by bulimic purging.

Michael Schiavo's statements concerning his wife's alleged eating disorder are all over the place. During his July 27, 1992, deposition for the malpractice trial, Michael claimed that Terri's weight fluctuated dramatically.

Q. Did she have any weight fluctuation—I'm talking between 4/87, which is your estimate of when you got here, and March of '90, did she have any weight fluctuation to any degree that you could see?

A. Yes.

Q. Okay. And what happened during that time?

A. She lost weight. What do you mean, what happened during that time?

Q. Well, she lost weight?

A. Uh-huh.

Q. Okay. How much weight?

A. Sometimes 20, 25 pounds.

Q. Was her weight fluctuating back and forth?

A. Yes.

Q. In other words, she'd lose 20, 25 pounds and she'd put some of it back on?

A. That's a guesstimate, 20, 25 pounds.

Q. Okay. Did she take it off and keep it off?

A. She put it back on; it would fluctuate.

Yet when presented with evidence that his wife's weight had not fluctuated so dramatically, Michael backpedaled from his prior testimony.

Q. Okay. According to my records, she saw [her general practitioner] four times, and her weight varied from 119—I'm sorry, from 120 to 123 and a half pounds, or three and a half pounds. Was she having a fluctuation in that period of time?

A. From what month to what month?

Q. I'm talking about from—let me see, from March—I'm sorry, yeah, from February 27, 1989, until February 2nd, 1990, she was weighed each time she went to see him, and—

A. So what was your question?

Q. My question is, did she have weight fluctuations during that period of time, that year before she had her attack?

A. I don't recall, I mean, any drastic fluctuations. I mean, I don't recall.

At several times throughout the deposition and subsequent trial testimony, Michael Schiavo stated that he had no indication that his wife was bulimic or had any kind of eating disorder. Here is one of those statements from his deposition.

Q. Do you have any indication yourself during all the time that you were dating and then married to Terri that she in any way was binging and purging?

A. I had no—no, none whatsoever.

And here is one from his November 5, 1992, testimony at the malpractice trial.

Q. And there was nothing about her appearance or anything about her which in any way, shape or form gave you any inclination that she had an eating disorder?

A. Nothing, no. No, none whatsoever.

Michael also testified that no one had ever mentioned to him that Terri might possibly have had an eating disorder.

In the January 24, 2000, trial over his guardianship of Terri, Michael Schiavo seems to distance himself even further from claims that his wife was bulimic.

Q. To your knowledge, while living with Terri, did you know whether or not she ever had an eating disorder such as anorexia or bulimia?

A. I did not. No. There was speculation made to that, but there was nothing ever proven in court as to that diagnosis.

Then, nearly three years later, in front of a national television audience, Michael appears to have come to the conclusion that his wife was bulimic.

LARRY KING: Was she bulimic?

SCHIAVO: When I was with her, when we were together, Terri would eat and eat and eat.

(CROSSTALK)

KING: . . . throwing up her meals?

SCHIAVO: Right. Bulimia, as from I've learned over the years, is a very secretive disease.

During the malpractice trial, Michael's lawyers Glenn Woodworth, Gary Fox, and Heather Harwell asked for $20 million in damages. Prior to the trial, Michael and the Schindler family discussed spending the money on either buying a house or building an addition onto the Schindler's house so that they could take Terri home and provide her with twenty-four-hour nursing care.

The malpractice jury reached a verdict on November 10, 1992, which was Michael and Terri's eighth wedding anniversary. They found for the plaintiffs, yet assigned Terri 70 percent of the blame and Dr. Igel 30 percent. Dr. Igel submitted all of the records pertaining to this case to the Florida Board of Medicine and was cleared of any professional malfeasance, and he continues his practice today. After the blame assignment and legal fees, Terri's estate received almost $1 million. This money was put into a trust to be managed by Michael, as her legal guardian. The trust would pay for Terri's medical care, although Michael could also make withdrawals from it for his own expenses and other costs associated with her care, such as legal fees. If Terri died, Michael would inherit the trust. In a separate award at the medical malpractice trial, Michael received approximately $400,000 (after legal fees and blame apportionment) for loss of consortium. I could not determine whether the $250,000 settlement from her general practitioner was placed in Terri's medical trust or given directly to Michael Schiavo. The fact that these records are sealed and controlled by Michael makes it difficult to know exactly what happened with these funds. Later guardians ad litem have found no financial improprieties on Michael's part. Michael was allowed to exercise a certain amount of discretion over the trust, for example, using it to pay legal fees in the dispute over guardianship and his efforts to have Terri's feeding tube removed.

If we look at the blame apportionment, it is clear that the jury didn't find Dr. Igel to be completely negligent. If the trial had been held today, with that blame apportionment, Michael and Terri's estate wouldn't have been awarded any money, since she was found to be responsible for more than half of the blame. Apparently, the jury found the plaintiff's case to be so heartbreaking that they gave her an award out of sympathy. Some time after the verdict, one of the jurors called Bobby Schindler and told him that they didn't like Michael Schiavo and didn't believe Terri was bulimic, but they gave her the award because they felt sorry for her.

Upon her admission to Humana Hospital, Terri's blood tests showed hypoglycemia and low protein levels. She had probably not been eating enough. Cardiac arrest from potassium imbalance brought on by bulimia and/or diuretic abuse is uncommon, and usually only occurs in extreme cases, which Terri doesn't seem to have been.

I think bulimia was a convenient hypothesis, because it laid the responsibility on the victim. It also is called a "secretive disease," and the women who suffer from it are often able to hide the symptoms from their family. How can a woman hide a serious and even life-threatening disease like bulimia from her husband and a very close family like the Schindlers? Personally, I don't think she was bulimic. She might have been malnourished, or suffering from some undiagnosed illness that lowered her potassium level, but the evidence supporting bulimia is thin at best.

POTASSIUM IMBALANCE

Whether or not Terri Schiavo suffered from bulimia, her potassium level was dangerously low upon admittance to Humana Hospital. Whatever the initial cause of her potassium imbalance, could this have caused her cardiac arrest?

The symptoms of severe potassium deficiency are:

Muscle cramps.
Weakness and paralysis.
Low blood pressure.
Rapid, irregular heartbeat.

Potassium deficiency is caused by:

Use of diuretic drugs.
Prolonged loss of bodily fluids through vomiting or
diarrhea.
Chronic kidney disease.

Uncontrolled diabetes.

Adrenal disease.

A dangerously low potassium level, or hypokalemia, usually occurs when someone loses a large amount of liquids, either through sweating, vomiting, or diarrhea. It is most frequently found in people who are taking diuretics, whether that medication is prescribed or they using it to lose weight quickly. Since diuretics promote urination, they reduce the level of fluid in the body, which can result in dehydration and loss of electrolytes (sodium, chloride, and potassium).

If Terri Schiavo had been losing fluids and electrolytes as a result of dehydration from excessive diuretics (iced tea, like coffee, is a diuretic), then the blood work upon her admission to Humana Hospital would have shown reduced levels of all electrolytes, not just potassium. Her sodium and chloride levels were normal.

Also, hypokalemia due to fluid loss is usually slight and temporary. The body can correct a short-term potassium imbalance without supplements or IVs. Foods such as bananas, oranges, and potatoes are rich in potassium. If a dangerously low potassium level is the result of fluid loss, that means prolonged diarrhea, accompanied by dehydration.

Potassium helps convert blood sugar into glycogen so that it can be stored in the muscles and liver to be released when necessary. Terri Schiavo was hypoglycemic upon admittance to the hospital. Her low blood sugar might have been caused by potassium deficiency. Potassium helps maintain the electrical charge in cells, allowing nerves and muscles to communicate. It is necessary to transport nutrients into cells and waste products out of them. Small changes in a potassium level can have adverse effects on nerve and muscle activity, particularly in the heart. Potassium can lead to an irregular heartbeat resulting in cardiac arrest.

While cardiac arrest due to potassium deficiency is uncommon, the deficiency itself is more prevalent than you might think. One in five people hospitalized in the United States has low potassium levels.

Whether or not it was the result of bulimia, Terri's potassium level was dangerously low and might have caused cardiac arrest. The potassium deficiency also might have rendered her more vulnerable to other stresses that could result in cardiac arrest. Even if it was never determined that her potassium deficiency—whether provoked by bulimia or not—was the direct cause of her cardiac arrest, we cannot exclude this as a possibility.

CHAPTER FIVE

Oxygen Deprivation

W e know Terri Schiavo suffered from oxygen deprivation to the brain for a period of several minutes. In order to better understand what could have happened to her, we need to take a closer look at oxygen deprivation and its causes.

Hypoxia is the deficiency of oxygen at the tissue level. Severe hypoxia of the brain is referred to as anoxia and is a reduction in oxygen supply to the brain. This is a relatively common cause of injury to the central nervous system. Prolonged brain anoxia may lead to brain death or a persistent vegetative state. The brain is the most oxygen-dependent organ in the human body. Some 25 to 30 percent of the oxygen we breathe goes to the brain, and if there is any oxygen deprivation, the brain will be the first organ to suffer damage.

Terri Schiavo's brain injury is described as anoxic encephalopathy. Encephalopathy is the general term used for any condition that affects the overall functioning of the brain. Lack of oxygen to the brain, severe infections, intoxication with drugs or alcohol, and liver and kidney failure are all common causes of this condition.

The doctors who examined Terri at Humana Hospital did not determine exactly what had deprived her brain of oxygen, although they thought it was probably cardiac arrest—whether the cause was low potassium level or something else. But we must consider another possibility: that oxygen deprivation provoked her collapse and cardiac arrest. Either her heart stopped first or the brain was deprived of oxygen through some external stimulus.

HOW DOES THE BRAIN GET DEPRIVED OF OXYGEN?

If Terri suffered cardiac arrest as a result of potassium deficiency, her heart either stopped beating, or beat so weakly that the oxygenated blood did not reach her brain. Brain damage began to occur when her brain was deprived of oxygen for approximately five to seven minutes. It is possible that her oxygen deprivation lasted longer than that. The doctors estimated that Terri's brain was without oxygen for eight minutes, but that is educated guesswork on their parts after seeing the extent of her brain damage.

The doctors at Humana diagnosed cardiac arrest because that is the condition in which the paramedics found Terri—more specifically cardiorespiratory arrest, because she wasn't breathing either. The cause of her cardiac arrest remains mysterious, or at best hypothetical. We have to explore the possibility that oxygen deprivation to her brain was the cause.

One possibility is that Terri's carotid blood flow, which supplies oxygen to the brain, was stopped for a long period of time. When this happens, the heart becomes oxygen-starved and ceases to beat. This could have occurred in the case of asphyxia, hanging, or strangulation.

ASPHYXIA

Asphyxia describes a lack of oxygen to the body. It is a very serious condition—if quick action is not taken, asphyxia will lead to unconsciousness and death.

There are several types of asphyxia, but I will only describe and discuss the four conditions that could possibly have provoked Terri's loss of oxygen.

1. *Compression asphyxia*. The loss of the ability to breathe due to outside forces placing pressure on the stomach or chest. This type could be as extreme as being crushed under a heavy object or as simple as someone sitting on a person's chest or stomach.

2. *Airway obstruction*. When oxygen is not able to reach the lungs because the airway is obstructed. There are four subcategories of airway obstruction.

    a. *Smothering*. The covering of the mouth or nose by a plastic bag, pillow, etc.
    b. *Gagging*. A gag is placed in the mouth and the tongue is pushed backward and upward; the gag becomes saturated with saliva and mucus, causing further obstruction.
    c. *Foreign-body obstruction*. An object—such as food, clothing, toys (those most at risk are infants and people with neurological difficulties)—obstructs the airway.
    d. *Swelling of the airway*. The mouth, thorax, or lungs swell because of allergic reaction or extreme heat.

3. *Cardiac arrhythmia*. Pressure over the carotid artery at the carotid sinus can provoke a reflex slowing of the heart (bradycardia), which may result in fatal arrhythmia. If the heart either stops or slows down enough, the rest of the body is deprived of oxygen.

4. *Mechanical constriction*. The most common mechanism is compression of the jugular veins and/or carotid arteries,

which leads to reduced oxygen reaching the brain, loss of consciousness, and if sustained for a significant time, death. Unconsciousness can occur in as few as ten seconds if both carotid arteries are compressed and in one minute if only the jugulars are compressed. Death occurs in minutes.

Pressure on both carotid arteries at once may also cause cardiac arrest and sudden cardiac death by activating a sensitive pressure receptor in the arteries that can stop the heart from beating.

Mechanical constriction also includes the limiting or blocking of air to the lungs, as in manual choking.

Considering Terri's case, the easiest of the above possibilities to eliminate is also the easiest to identify: airway obstruction. There has never been any indication from the medical record or witnesses that Terri was choking. Once paramedics arrived, they began CPR, first establishing an airway and then compressing the chest. There were no notations by paramedics, either written or verbal, that upon their arrival and subsequent emergency medical treatment, an airway obstruction was encountered.

It is possible that Terri suffered minor airway obstruction if she had recently vomited and some of the vomit remained in her throat. Yet if this had caused her to suffocate, we would have seen it in the medical evidence and hospital reports. One year after her collapse, Michael Schiavo told Dr. James Carnahan at Mediplex Rehabilitation Hospital in Bradenton that he found some vomit near Terri after she collapsed, but later determined that it belonged to one of their cats. I will deal with this statement in more detail later, but mention it now to point out that it is the only mention in the voluminous medical records that I have studied of vomit or any other possible airway obstruction (which is curious in a case of alleged bulimia).

While there is no way to completely eliminate the possibility of airway constriction, we must conclude that it is very remote. Yes, an obstruction could have constricted Terri's breathing and never been found. She could have choked on something and coughed it up. The paramedics could have cleared her airway of an obstruction during CPR, not realizing that this was the cause of her collapse.

One method of airway constriction is suicide by a plastic bag wrapped around the head. Sometimes the person who finds the body will remove the bag to spare the victim and her family from the stigma of suicide. But there is no indication that this occurred. No bag was found at or near the scene and Terri did not exhibit any conduct consistent with suicidal tendencies or even depression. Possibilities such as a suicide attempt must be explored, even if only to be eliminated.

A method of asphyxia that is consistent with the evidence in this case is asphyxia resulting in cardiac arrhythmia. This is an irregular heartbeat caused by outside forces such as pressure placed on the carotid artery at the carotid sinus, provoking bradycardia, a very slow heartbeat that can be fatal. Stress, hypertension, or other debilitating conditions including low potassium could be contributing factors to cardiac arrhythmia secondary to pressure on both carotid arteries simultaneously. The medical records show that upon resuscitation, Terri suffered from tachycardia, an increased heartbeat. Yet bradycardia can trigger cardiac arrest. Then, once the heart starts beating again, its rhythm is much faster because it is trying to catch up.

At first glance, compression asphyxia might not seem possible in this case because it often involves the victim being crushed by a heavy object, such as in a building collapse or vehicle accident. Yet sometimes the force does not have to be so traumatic. All that is necessary is enough pressure placed against someone's chest or stomach that respiration is stopped or impaired. Without respiration, the heart cannot pump oxygenated blood to the brain. The person loses consciousness and, if deprived of oxygen long enough, suffers brain damage and even death.

Compression asphyxia can be the result of an unintentional act or an intentional act that never has the victim's death as a goal. Example: Kids are playing and everyone engages in the "dog pile." The person on the bottom could be in such a position that respiration is impossible because of the pressure exerted on the abdomen and chest. The longer the period of time the person is without respiration, the greater the chance of rendering him unconscious.

Here's another example, closer to the conditions surrounding Terri's collapse. Terri's family claims that Terri told them that Michael would roughhouse with her. Suzanne described him doing the same to her. If Michael was roughhousing with Terri and fell on Terri's back with his full weight of two hundred forty pounds, with Terri landing on the hard surface of the floor and his weight compressing her chest, she may have been unable to breathe. The combination of the aforementioned cardiac arrhythmia (pressure on the carotid causing an irregular and slow heartbeat) that a compression could cause and her low potassium level, whether or not it caused cardiac arrest, might have contributed to the stress on Terri's heart. There could be a multicausal explanation for Terri's collapse, i.e., a series of separate events and conditions combining at the right time to bring about near-fatal cardiac arrest.

Accidents happen. They are a part of everyday life. Conduct that is innocent and without malicious intent can have no criminality except negligence attached even if the act is so dangerous that the person should have understood the risks. But once an accident occurs and the involved party fails to explain and describe the events accurately, the victim might not receive timely or specific treatment soon enough. The failure of the involved parties to be honest about the events that led to the injury are usually motivated by the guilt or fear that they feel, holding themselves responsible for the victim's injury or death. At least, sometimes they are.

Another possibility, even more troubling, is mechanical constriction. This is usually described in a criminal sense, but we must not forget that no matter how dangerous this conduct or force is, mechanical constriction can sometimes begin as innocent, though reckless, behavior. The fact that this behavior is concealed, lied about, or denied only contributes to suspicion, even if the act was not committed with intent to injure or kill.

The only one reason to discuss this before looking at the criminal aspects of mechanical constriction is to make the reader aware that noncriminal explanations can exist for what often appears to be an intentional act.

Strangulation is asphyxia caused by closure of the blood vessels and/or air passages of the neck as a result of external pressure.

There are three types of strangulation: hanging, ligature, and manual. We can eliminate hanging and ligature because there is no evidence that a rope or other object—such as a towel or piece of clothing—was used. Both hanging and ligature strangulation leave marks on the victim's neck, and there was no evidence of any such marks on Terri.

Manual strangulation is usually done with the hands. Different variations involve the forearms (as in police carotid choke holds) or standing on or kneeling on the victim's throat.

WHAT HAPPENS WHEN SOMEONE IS STRANGLED?

Manual strangulation involves the external compression of the neck, cutting off blood circulation to the head. The airway may also be closed off, resulting in an inability to breathe. The process of a person dying by strangulation is one of severe pain followed by unconsciousness and brain damage and ultimately death. Methods of strangulations include:

1. *Closing off airway.* The trachea is externally compressed to the point where the lungs are deprived of oxygen. After fifty seconds of continuous oxygen deprivation, the victim rarely recovers without medical assistance.

2. *Blocking off carotid arteries.* These are the arteries on either side of the neck that carry oxygenated blood from the heart to the brain. If one or both of the carotid arteries are compressed, such as by a carotid choke hold—where the victim's neck is compressed in the crook of his attacker's elbow—the flow of oxygenated blood from the heart to the brain is restricted, and the brain is deprived of oxygen.

3. *Blocking off jugular veins.* These are the two veins that transport deoxygenated blood from the brain down to the heart. If the jugular veins are compressed, the victim will suffer lack of oxygen to the brain because the deoxygenated blood is not able to return to the heart, preventing oxygenated blood from going to the brain.

Any combination of these injuries can occur at the same time. Often in strangulation cases, there is more than one compression point. The force necessary to accomplish these deadly results is minimal. It takes only eleven pounds of pressure placed on the carotid arteries for ten seconds to render a victim unconscious. If released immediately, they should revive without assistance in about ten seconds. To completely close off the trachea requires thirty-three pounds of pressure, or three times the amount necessary for carotid strangulation.

When the airway is cut off by manual strangulation, it takes four to five minutes for the victim to die. This kind of strangulation is very difficult to inflict upon a conscious victim without some signs of a struggle, either on the part of victim or suspect.

Aside from the direct wounds to the hyoid bone and trachea, the victim might have skin or blood beneath her fingernails. The suspect might have scratch marks or hair pulled out. Both parties could exhibit bruising from their struggle. Because of the length of time necessary to kill someone by manual airway constriction, it is often considered first-degree murder, since the suspect has time to premeditate his act and its consequences during the strangulation itself.

In order to determine whether or not death was caused by strangulation, forensic pathologists look for the following signs.

Damage to the hyoid bone. One of the common injuries one finds in strangulation deaths is damage to the small horseshoe-shaped bone in the neck that helps support the tongue. This is called the hyoid bone. In cases of manual strangulation where the trachea is compressed, the hyoid bone is usually broken, since it requires much force to close the trachea. The exception is victims younger than age thirty, whose hyoid bones might not break because the two halves of the bone have not yet fused.

Damage to the larynx. The larynx is made up of the thyroid cartilage and the tracheal rings. In the case of manual strangulation cutting off oxygen to the lungs, you will usually find damage to the larynx and trachea.

Petechial hemorrhage. Tiny red spots due to ruptured capillaries. They are usually found around the eyes, under the eyelids, or anywhere on the face or neck above the area of constriction. A particularly violent struggle between the assailant and victim may result in bloodred eyes as a result of a rupture of the capillaries in the white part of the eye. While petechial hemorrhage is found in the vast majority of cases of manual strangulation, there can be manual strangulation without petechial hemorrhages observed even in some victims who died from the stangulation itself. And petechial hemorrhage will not be seen in cases of cardiac arrhythmia due to bradycardia caused by pressure over the carotid artery, because the heart stopped beating first.

Lung damage and aspiration pneumonitis. This evidence is frequently overlooked during investigations of strangulation cases. During the strangulation, the victim may inhale vomit into her lungs, which could lead to aspiration pneumonitis, where the gastric acids begin to digest the lung tissue. Milder cases of pneumonia may also occur hours or days later. Terri Schiavo suffered pneumonia shortly after being admitted to Humana Hospital, although it is impossible to determine whether her illness was a side effect of strangulation or had some other cause, such as infection during CPR airway treatment, tracheostomy, or a preexisting condition.

Involuntary urination and defecation. Strangulation victims usually void themselves at or near death. Bobby did not notice any stains or smell when he saw Terri. There are no remarks in the medical records I have examined to the effect that she voided her bowels or bladder.

Following an attempted strangulation, victims may exhibit the following symptoms: voice changes such as hoarseness or complete loss of voice; difficulty or pain in swallowing; difficulty or pain in breathing; psychosis or amnesia.

Terri Schiavo exhibited no outward signs of airway constriction. Her face and neck were not bruised. While the police may not have conducted a thorough investigation of the scene, there were no visible signs of a struggle. No one noticed any scratches or bruises on Michael Schiavo. I think we can safely eliminate manual airway constriction as a possible manner of death in this case.

Carotid and jugular constriction are more difficult to prove or disprove. Unless there was a violent struggle, petechial hemorrhages may be the only marks left on the victim's body. Yet sometimes petechial hemorrhages are very subtle and go unobserved, particularly if the victim survives the strangulation attempt. They may also be misidentified or not identified at all by the doctor. And petechial hemorrhage does not manifest itself in every manual-strangulation case. According to a study conducted by Dr. Vincent DeMaio, one of the nation's leading forensic pathologists, petechial hemorrhage was noted in 89 percent of manual-strangulation deaths.

Manual constriction of the carotid arteries or jugular veins poses serious challenges to homicide investigators. Most victims are female and their assailants are male. Many of these cases involve domestic abuse. When the victim dies, it is often difficult to find physical evidence of strangulation. And even when the victim lives, she is often reluctant to press charges, or even tell the truth to investigators, because she wishes to protect her partner or is afraid of retaliation.

Dr. George McClane is an emergency-room doctor and director of the Forensic Medical Unit for the Family Justice Center, a domestic-abuse agency for the city of San Diego. McClane is a leading authority on strangulation in domestic-abuse cases. After studying three hundred attempted strangulation cases with female victims who were assaulted by their partners, McClane and Assistant City Attorney Gael Strack found that 89 percent of the cases involved a history of domestic violence. Most victims lacked physical evidence of being strangled. They either had no visible injury (50 percent) or their injuries were too minor to photograph (35 percent). These minor injuries included redness on the neck and small cuts or scratches. Visible injuries were found in only 15 per-

cent of the cases. These red marks may or may not darken to become a bruise. In only 3 percent of the cases McClane studied did
the victims seek medical attention, and these were primarily to
treat the secondary effects of strangulation, such as persistent
pain, voice changes, or trouble swallowing.

> *"Strangulation has only recently been identified as one of the
> most lethal forms of domestic violence. When perpetrators use
> strangulation to silence their victims, this is a form of power and
> control that has a devastating psychological effect on victims
> and a potentially fatal outcome. Historically, 'choking' was
> rarely prosecuted as a serious offense because victims minimize
> the level of violence and police and medical personnel fail to
> recognize it."*
>
> —GAEL B. STRACK AND DR. GEORGE MCCLANE,
> *HOW TO IMPROVE YOUR INVESTIGATION AND
> PROSECUTION OF STRANGULATION CASES*

Domestic-violence strangulation is a big problem in the United
States, and one that doesn't get much attention—probably because there is so little physical evidence left on the victims,
whether alive or dead. Ten percent of violent deaths in the United
States each year are due to strangulation, with six female victims
to every male. In 70 to 80 percent of all domestic-violence cases,
the victim will recant. Medical personnel often fail to recognize
that a patient is a strangulation victim. Some victims of manual
strangulation show no visible injuries, yet some rare cases cause
brain damage that worsens daily, resulting in death even weeks
later.

WAS TERRI SCHIAVO STRANGLED?

Strangulation deaths are difficult to prove even when the victim is dead and autopsied shortly after the assault. In a case where the victim lay in a comalike state for fifteen years, and an investigator must rely on hospital records and witness reports, it is nearly impossible to reach a determination just from the medical evidence.

There has been some controversy, and a great deal of speculation, that the stiffness evident in Terri's neck, even in the last year of her life, is proof that she might have been strangled. If we look at the medical records, we note that some early reports describe Terri's neck as being "somewhat stiff." Other reports from the same time describe her neck as being "supple." There were no observed neck injuries when she was first admitted.

> KING: What about charges you abused her?
>
> SCHIAVO: The Schindlers made accusations that I
> strangled Terri. It confuses me, because before any of
> this came to light, don't you think the doctors at
> solitary [sic], when it first happened, would notice
> marks around her neck? And if I strangled her to the
> point of unconsciousness, her trachea would have
> been crushed.
>
> — *LARRY KING LIVE,* OCTOBER 27, 2003

That's not necessarily true, as a carotid choke hold would not necessarily have resulted in a crushed trachea or marks around the neck. Michael Schiavo could have given Terri a carotid choke hold, depriving her brain of oxygen and causing cardiac arrest. In fact, Mary Schindler told me she saw Michael grab his brother Scott in that manner during a fight. Could he have grabbed Terri that way, either during the course of a domestic dispute or in "horseplay"? It is possible, but based on the available medical evidence, I can make no determination either way.

CHAPTER SIX

The Bone Scan

One piece of evidence that has generated a great deal of suspicion that Terri's collapse might have been the result of domestic abuse at the hands of her husband is a bone scan conducted in March 1991 and not discovered by the Schindlers until November 2002.

When the Schindlers found the bone-scan report that stated "This patient has a history of trauma" and described what appeared to be multiple fractures in several different places, they feared that Terri had been abused by Michael, either before, during, or after her collapse. Terri had not had a broken bone in her life, and the bone scan only showed fractures that had occurred up to twelve to eighteen months prior to the test. Also in November 2002, the Schindlers learned that Terri had been visited by an orthopedic surgeon at Humana Hospital on May 6, 1990, just three days prior to her discharge. Michael Schiavo never told the family about that consultation or that Terri was expressing physical discomfort in March 1991, or that a bone scan had been conducted.

They filed an emergency motion before circuit-court judge George Greer, who had presided over much of the Schindler–Schiavo litigation. The Schindlers' motion asked for a full evidentiary hearing, which Greer denied. "The court concludes," Greer wrote, "that while it might be interesting to pursue the issue of trauma as it may have occurred almost twelve years ago, that has nothing to do with Theresa Marie Schiavo in 2002" and the court's mandate.

So the bone scan and other evidence, including affidavits from doctors who had examined the record, were never fully considered by the court.

WHAT DOES THE BONE SCAN SAY?

The bone scan had been ordered in March 1991 by Dr. James Carnahan, Terri's rehabilitation physician at Mediplex. Dr. Carnahan asked the radiology department at Manatee Memorial Hospital to "evaluate for trauma." Terri had been showing signs that she was experiencing pain and her doctors could not identify its possible source. The specific request to "evaluate for trauma" could be a suggestive indicator to the doctor performing the bone scan of any irregularities linked to trauma.

Of course, trauma does not necessarily mean violence. It could be the result of injuries that are organic or accidental.

HOW DOES A BONE SCAN WORK?

The physician injects the patient with a radioactive material, then waits three hours before placing the patient under an imaging camera that can record the radioactive material as it decays. This radioactive material acts the same as the calcium and phosphate in the bone. Since the skeletal system is an ever-changing and self-repairing system, the body is constantly sending new material to build and maintain the bones. This is a normal process called bone turnover.

When the bone turnover is abnormal, either lots of bone is being removed and not much put back or more bone is being deposited than is being removed. When radioactive material is introduced prior to a bone scan, the body thinks the radioactive material is the same as bone material and processes it in the same way. In this manner, the radioactive material "piggybacks" onto the calcium and phosphate and goes where repairs are in process. These abnormal areas show up as black in a bone scan because a significant amount of the radioactive material is sent to that location, indicating areas of healing activity. An area of healing activity could mean a process of healing or cell replacement in excess of the normal maintenance and rebuilding.

Dr. Campbell Walker was called in to perform and evaluate the bone scan. The report was reviewed by Dr. Florence Heimberg, his associate in the radiology department. They also took a series of X-rays to refine the diagnosis. Since the bone scan is a measure of the body's metabolism, the X-ray gives a picture of a bone that doesn't involve any metabolic processes that might be occurring at that time. The X-ray is more static. However, bone scans can give a more accurate reading of how old any bone abnormalities such as fractures might be, and narrow down the time window in which any damage to specific bones might have occurred. Typically, a fracture can be seen on a bone scan for twelve to eighteen months.

The test found "an extensive number of focal abnormal areas." Here are the areas where Dr. Walker found increased metabolic activity indicating previous trauma.

1. *Multiple bilateral ribs.* More than two ribs, on both sides.

2. *Costovertebral aspects of several of the thoracic vertebral bodies.* Where the rear part of the rib joins the spine.

3. *L1 vertebral body.* A vertebra in the small of the back. The five lumbar vertebrae bear much of the body's weight.

4. *Sacroiliac C joints.* Where the pelvis connects to the spine at the sacrum.

5. *Right femoral diaphysis.* The shaft of the right leg bone above the knee.

6. Both knees and both ankles.

Some of these injuries are less serious and might not be connected to Terri's collapse or any suspected abuse before or after. The trauma to both ankles and knees could not be life threatening at the time of her collapse or anytime thereafter. The increased bone activity could be due to the fact that she had been bedridden for more than a year and her joints were beginning to fuse.

There seems to be some confusion between abnormalities and fractures. In his deposition, Dr. Walker stated that the darkened areas in the bone scan show increased activity consistent with bone repair, but cannot be described as fractures unless corroborated through other sources such as X-rays. While X-rays were taken of some of the areas showing possible trauma, they were not taken of all areas.

POSSIBLE RIB FRACTURES

The bone-scan report notes that there were areas of abnormality on bilateral posterior of the rib cage, close to where the ribs are attached to the vertebrae. Unfortunately, neither the bone scan report nor Dr. Walker's deposition described exactly which ribs had been fractured and where those fractures were located, only that they were in the back. In his deposition, Walker stated that when multiple ribs are involved bilaterally the report usually does not identify ribs by number.

The doctors at Humana Hospital took an X-ray of Terri's chest the morning she was admitted, but made no notations of any fractures or abnormalities to the rib cage. Humana doctors were looking for abnormalities in the lungs and heart—not broken bones.

Did Terri Schiavo suffer multiple rib fractures? The medical record is not clear and we probably will never know whether Terri's ribs were fractured or to what degree. Dr. Walker did not order chest X-rays in order to determine whether the activity he noted on the bone scan was due to recent fractures.

Q. Can you tell from your report whether you ordered X-rays of her ribs?

A. I would say that those were not ordered. We don't do all areas of abnormality if the areas on the bone scan are so extensive, because, as you know, there's radiation involved, and you want to minimize the amount of radiation to patients.

Q. So we don't know whether her ribs were broken?

A. We don't.

— DR. W. CAMPBELL WALKER,
DEPOSITION, NOVEMBER 21, 2003

Dr. Michael Baden, one of the most respected forensic pathologists in the country, reviewed the bone scan and the report. He told me that "a bone scan is not the best way to look for fractures." What the bone scan can do, Dr. Baden said, is to indicate areas where fractures could possibly have occurred. "You can get these accumulations on bone scans that are false alarms," Dr. Baden said, "but they tell you where you should take the X-rays." The X-rays will help determine whether the activity indicates fractures or other bone turnover. Earlier X-rays from the patient's medical records can be examined in order to see if fractures existed—or not.

From the bone scan and Humana Hospital X-rays, we don't know if Terri's ribs were fractured. Even if they were, this trauma could have occurred during the resuscitation measures.

Terri was defibrillated seven times. That means a successful heartbeat had not been obtained by at least one initial attempt at CPR. Also, in between each defibrillation, manual CPR was used. Bobby Schindler remembers the paramedics applying CPR as his sister was being taken down the stairs toward the ambulance, and it's not a stretch to imagine that such vigorous resuscitation attempts continued while en route to the hospital. That means Terri had repeated CPR compressions to her sternum at least seven times (once before initial defibrillation, once between each defibrillation, once on the way to the ambulance) and probably more.

Terri Schiavo was five foot four and weighed one hundred and twenty pounds. The force of the pressure the paramedics exerted on her sternum in order to revive her heartbeat could very easily have resulted in these fractures. According to one study, CPR results in rib fractures in 28 percent of adult patients. However, during CPR, the area of fractures most often reported is usually located anteriorily, or in layman's terms, in the front. These fractures are fairly close to the sternum, which in 16 percent of the adult patients also shows damage.

Terri's fractures are in the back. Sometimes ribs can break at a point other than direct impact, as a tree branch can snap off nearer the trunk if you pull on one end. Yet CPR fractures are the result of direct pressure on the front of the ribs near the sternum.

When asked if bilateral injuries to the ribs could have been caused by CPR, Walker replied: "A vigorous resuscitation could do that, yes."

Dr. Baden agreed that it was possible Terri suffered rib fractures during resuscitation, yet "they were posterior, which made it much less likely that it could have been done by CPR."

The rib fractures—if that's what they were—are also consistent with someone falling on top of her from behind.

L1 VERTEBRA

"The activity in L1 correlates perfectly with the compression fracture which is presumably traumatic."

—BONE-SCAN REPORT, MARCH 5, 1991

In the bone scan, the first lumbar vertebra showed abnormal activity, which was corroborated by an X-ray as being the result of a compression fracture—in other words, a broken back. Compression fractures involve pushing down with force onto a vertebra to the point of damaging the mechanical structure of that bone.

The lumbar region of the spine carries a great portion of the body's weight and experiences related biomechanical stress. This area of the spine is most commonly called the small of the back. The cartilages in between the vertebrae act as the body's shock absorbers. Sometimes they absorb a shock that is too great and the bone structure of one or more vertebrae is damaged along the end plates, the portions of the vertebrae adjacent to the cartilages that separate each vertebral body.

Compression fractures to lumbar vertebrae are rather common injuries. They can be caused by paragliding, falling off a ladder, a car accident, or any other trauma in which the body is jolted along the spinal column, particularly in landing on the rear end. It is not a common injury in domestic abuse, unless the victim falls down as the result of violence.

Just an hour after she arrived at Humana Hospital, Terri was given diagnostic imaging (the documents do not note whether this was X-ray or MRI), which found no vertebral bone damage.

> *Single Cross Table Lateral Portable View of Cervical Spine 8:00 AM 2-25-90*
>
> *There is no evidence of vertebral compression or of acute bony destructive changes.*
>
> *Impression: No Acute Bony Pathology*

Terri suffered multiple and uncontrollable seizures after and probably before the image was taken at 8:00 A.M. During one of her seizure episodes, it is possible that she suffered a compression fracture of the L1 vertebra. It is also possible that she fell from her bed at some point when the side rails were down. Another possibility is that Terri was injured during transport, or during routine care or therapy, and the injury was never reported. During the period between Terri's initial admission to Humana and the bone scan, she had been transported to College Harbor nursing home, a month later moved to Bayfront Center, then to the Schindlers' home, back to College Harbor nursing home, flown to University of California at San Francisco for experimental brain implants, and flown back home again before being admitted to Mediplex.

The L1 compression fracture is most probably connected to the abnormal activity noted in the sacroiliac joints (small joints where the pelvis meets the spine), which showed abnormalities but no fractures. Considering the fact that both sides of the sacroiliac showed signs of trauma, I would tend to think that these injuries were connected to the compression fracture of the first lumbar vertebra. The sacroiliac joints connect the spine to the pelvis and it is certainly possible that the force of a compression fracture to L1 could also have caused injury to both sacroiliac joints.

The bilateral damage in Terri's sacroiliac joints suggest the possibility of some accident, possibly while she was being transported.

RIGHT LEG

The bone scan showed an abnormality in the right femur that could have indicated a fracture. The X-ray did not show a fracture, but did show a periosteal reaction, which is a bone injury with no loss of bone continuity. The common name is a bone bruise.

Dr. Walker described this injury as not very likely to have occurred as a result of falling to the floor during a cardiac arrest.

> *"Typically you need a direct blow of some kind. I suppose one could speculate that she fell on a piece of furniture, that that could produce that injury. But just typically falling on the floor would not do that."*
>
> —DR. W. CAMPBELL WALKER, DEPOSITION,
> NOVEMBER 21, 2003

Walker also said that the injury was not the result of a joint injury possibly inflicted in physical therapy, because joint injuries do not typically show up on bone scans.

Q. Would a kick be the kind of direct blow that would produce that femoral abnormality?

A. That would be a possibility, yes.

Q. Would being thrown into a sharp furniture corner?

A. That would be a possibility.

Q. Would being struck with some sort of blunt object like a golf club or something to do it?

A. Yes.

This line of questioning is an example of how some people have used the bone scan to try to prove that Michael abused Terri. Whether he did or not, the bone scan does not prove it, and other evidence indicates that the trauma indicated by the bone scan probably occurred after her collapse.

When Terri was examined upon admittance to Humana Hospital, doctors noted no edema (or blood swelling) in her extremities. Her right knee was X-rayed just prior to her discharge on May 9, 1990.

> *The bones comprising the right knee are intact with no fracture, dislocation or other focal bony abnormality.*
> *Impression: No Bony Abnormality*
> *Diagnostic Imaging Report 5-5-90*

The bone scan was performed thirteen months after Terri's collapse. Considering the fact that doctors thought a bone scan was necessary in order to identify any abnormalities and possible trauma, I think it's safe to assume that if Terri had suffered any fracture on or prior to February 25, 1990, by the time of the bone scan it would have been healed to the degree that the fracture would not be visible on the X-ray.

WHAT DOES THE BONE SCAN SAY?

Terri Schiavo suffered multiple traumas around the time of her collapse. These traumas very possibly could have been caused by her collapse itself, treatments immediately afterward, and/or the seizures she experienced later that morning. The bone scan does not prove that these traumas were caused by violence or that she was physically abused. She had never had a broken bone and appeared to her family, who saw her regularly, to be in good health.

She had not been in a car accident. There were no prior hospitalizations for trauma.

It is highly unlikely that these traumas were the result of domestic violence prior to her collapse. Terri would not have been able to hide the effects of fractured ribs from her family and coworkers. Besides, beatings usually don't result in bilateral rib fractures. Instead, you'll see fractures on one side, where the assailant hits the victim with his hand or a weapon.

Considered together, the traumas shown on the bone scan do not seem to be related. They were probably caused by separate events. In domestic abuse, you will see recurring injuries, such as a fractured cheekbone from a punch, or a series of related injuries, such as when the victim falls down a flight of stairs.

If it is impossible to nail down the precise time when these traumas occurred, we know it was within a twelve- to eighteen-month period prior to March 5, 1991. The L1 compression fracture might have occurred prior to or during Terri's collapse, and the imaging missed it. The bone bruise on her right femur might also have occurred during her collapse, but not being a fracture, it was not picked up by the X-ray of her right knee. The rib fractures could possibly have been caused at her collapse by someone falling on top of her from behind.

Yet there is no medical proof to precisely determine the time or nature of these traumas. The bone-scan report cannot stand alone as evidence of abuse or assault.

CHAPTER SEVEN

Money, Sex, Power

The medical evidence offers a small number of possibilities to explain Terri's collapse, yet does not offer any proof that it was the result of natural causes or homicide. At this point, her death is unexplained, which means we must explore the possibility of a criminal act. In order to do so, I will examine Terri's life up until her collapse, to see if that provides any clues, focusing on those aspects of her personal history that can shed some light on whether or not she was a victim of domestic abuse and whether her relationship with Michael could have escalated into violence.

There are three things that usually provoke violent reactions in intimate relationships: money, sex, and power.

MONEY

When Terri first met Michael, she was driving a black-and-gold Firebird that her father had leased for his business and let her drive most of the time. She dressed well and lived in an affluent neighborhood. Michael's family had less money, his father worked for GTE, and they lived in Levittown, one of the first housing tracts built after World War II.

When they were married, Terri and Michael received about

$10,000 to $15,000 in cash gifts. They moved into a rented town house not far from the Schindlers. Soon they couldn't afford the rent. Terri asked her parents if she and Michael could move in with them, living rent-free. At this time, Terri had her job at Prudential and Michael was working as a McDonald's manager.

One day Terri showed her father an expensive-looking watch.

"Dad, take a look at this," she said. "Mike is buying this for one of the employees who is leaving the McDonald's. Isn't that strange?"

"You'd better keep your eye on that boy," her father said.

When the Schindlers decided to move down to Florida, Terri asked if she and Michael could go with them. Terri and Michael moved to Florida in April 1986, ahead of her parents. They stayed in the Schindlers' condo while the Schindlers bought a house. The Schindlers also helped them with moving costs. After living in the condo for two years, Terri and Michael moved into a one-bedroom apartment at Thunder Bay Apartments in North St. Petersburg in 1988, helped by another loan from the Schindlers. Terri and Michael consolidated their credit-card bills because they were overextended.

> *"She's a big family person, and she really appreciated what they were doing. But Michael wasn't working. This was not what she wanted out of a marriage."*
>
> —JACKIE RHODES

While Michael had expensive tastes, often buying designer suits when he and Terri were having trouble paying the rent, Terri earned the bulk of their income. She began working for Prudential a few months prior to their marriage. Except for a brief period when she waited for a transfer shortly after relocating to Florida, she remained employed.

Michael Schiavo's employment history is more spotty. He

worked as a manager at a series of restaurants, but he was frequently unemployed. Michael has claimed in testimony and in a job application to have been continually employed during this time, but all Terri's families and friends dispute this. In his medical malpractice deposition, Michael exaggerated his work history so much that the defense attorney pointed out that if he added up all the years Michael claimed to have worked at various jobs, they would end up sometime well into the future.

"He always had trouble with his jobs. Everybody was always wrong and he was right."

—MARY SCHINDLER

Several of Terri's colleagues at Prudential remember that Michael's frequent unemployment was difficult for her. When he was working, Michael would call her at the office and complain about his job. She would get very upset during these phone calls and often cried afterward. During one phone call, Michael threatened to quit his job. Terri begged him not to. When she came in to work the next day, Terri told her friends that he had quit. She wasn't happy about it.

And when Terri spent eighty dollars on her haircolor, Michael got angry and they had a fight.

SEX

Michael Schiavo was the first man Terri ever kissed. She went to a coed Catholic high school where the boys and girls were kept separate. She didn't have any experience with boys. Being overweight made her self-conscious and shy. Then, once she lost the weight, she met Michael.

After Terri's collapse, Michael said that they had been trying to have a baby. Terri had been having infrequent menstruation and had been to see an OB-GYN, who prescribed progesterone. Terri wasn't on birth control and she never conceived. Michael testified that they had used condoms before they decided to have children several months prior to her collapse. None of her family members recall her saying that Michael and she were trying to have a baby.

"I thought she told me everything," Mary says, "but she hadn't mentioned children."

Terri's obstetrician-gynecologist was the defendant in the medical malpractice suit. So it is possible that the stated desire to have children was part of the strategy to raise the award level. If Terri's collapse prevented the couple from having children, the jury might feel sympathy and possibly award more money.

Jackie Rhodes remembers that when Dr. Igel wanted Michael to give a sperm sample for a fertility test, he refused, "because that was something he just didn't want to do." (Michael has fathered two children with his fiancée, Jodi Centonze, so apparently infertility wasn't the problem.)

> *"Terri used to say to me that sometimes she would almost have to beg him for sex. He would not want to be intimate. It used to upset her. She was disappointed."*
>
> —MARY SCHINDLER

POWER

People who knew him in different places and at different times have told me exactly the same thing: "Michael was very controlling." This is said by Terri's friends and family, but also by Michael's former girlfriends and nurses who didn't know Terri prior to her collapse. It is described in details that corroborate the statements of different witnesses who did not know one another. And these statements have been sworn to in affidavits and verified to me, and other investigators, during interviews.

Michael's control manifested itself early in their relationship. According to Terri's friends, Michael obsessed over even the smallest details of the wedding. Diane Meyer remembers him choosing the flowers and even going to the dress store with the bridesmaids to help select their gowns.

> "Michael was the most involved groom I had ever seen. The wedding was all about him."
>
> — DIANE MEYER

Terri got along well with Michael's family, becoming very close to his sisters-in-law and brothers. His mother, Claire, loved Terri, who was like the daughter she never had.

"Sometimes I swear she married Michael because of his family," Mary told me. "She and her sisters-in-law were like sisters. She loved Michael's family."

She was so close to his brother Brian, and her own family liked him better than Michael, leading them to say, "Too bad you didn't marry Brian."

The first time Terri met the Schiavo family was an awkward experience. Toward the end of a family gathering in the Schiavo backyard, all five brothers stood on the picnic table and had a contest to see who could urinate the farthest. Everyone was there, including their parents and grandmother. It seemed to be fairly normal behavior for the five brothers. Terri had invited Diane Meyer along as moral support. On the ride home, Diane asked Terri if she was sure she wanted to marry into that family.

"Yeah, they're a little outrageous at times," Terri replied, laughing it off.

The friends Terri had before she started seeing Michael were not convinced the marriage was a good idea. She was taken aside on several occasions by girlfriends and even by her brother, Bobby, to make sure she knew what she was doing. They were afraid that things were happening too quickly, and Terri didn't have the experience to know any better.

"Terri was such an incredible person that we all felt that if she was in love with him, there must have been some good in him," Diane told me. "She was so good and so special that you wanted to believe that good was going to happen to her."

Robert Schindler remembers hearing Michael yell at Terri when they were living in the basement of their Pennsylvania home. In St. Petersburg, Michael was often alone in the apartment during the day while Terri worked, whether he was working nights or unemployed. His mother told Mary Schindler that he was having a hard time being alone in the apartment while Terri was at work.

Muriel Wechstrum remembers one night when she invited Terri and Michael over for dinner. They came separately, and Michael arrived a half hour before Terri, who was running late.

Michael was "furious," according to Muriel. "How dare she keep me waiting?" he said.

Another time, Muriel took Terri to the zoo, and when Michael found out about it, he became "furious jealous," in Muriel's words, "because he wanted to take her."

"Michael was disrespectful, condescending. A bully to me and to Terri," Suzanne says, remembering how she would talk to Terri about Michael. "She would say, 'I know he's a jerk.' Then she would blow it off. Terri was passive, she kept a lot of stuff inside."

"Terri would never come out and tell him what she wanted," her mother recalls. If Terri wanted to go to the movies, she would tell Michael, "If you want to go to the movies, I wouldn't mind," instead of expressing her wishes directly.

"She had been teased about her weight throughout her teen years, and I know for a fact that Terri was very insecure about herself. Terri was extremely timid, and this continued even after she and Michael moved to St. Petersburg. As a child and an adult, she was an easy person to dominate, not prone to standing up for herself."

— BOBBY SCHINDLER, AFFIDAVIT, AUGUST 24, 2003

Sue Pickwell remembers that prior to their marriage, Terri told her that Michael was upset because she was starting to gain weight.

"Terri was the sweetest person ever," Sue told investigators, "and Michael was claiming that he loved her, but saying negative things."

Jackie Rhodes remembers Terri telling her that one day Michael saw a picture of when she was heavy and said: "If you ever get fat, I'll divorce you."

When she was heavier, Terri would cry to her mother about her weight. Even after she took the weight off, she remained very sensitive about it.

Michael never really connected with the Schindlers, except for Mary, during the first couple of years following Terri's collapse. The Schindler family is exceptionally close and spends a lot of time together. Michael would attend family functions, but he didn't socialize with them as much as Terri did. Often she would come over to visit her parents without Michael, whether or not he was working. And Michael and Terri rarely went out together.

Terri and Michael owned two cars, a secondhand Olds Cutlass and a new Nissan Pulsar. Terri drove the Nissan to work, but Michael often checked the odometer to see how far she had driven it. (He has denied this in testimony; all of her family and several coworkers remember Terri telling them he did.) If she was going to visit her parents, Michael would tell her that he knew the exact mileage between the two houses, and she better not go anywhere else. When the girls from the office went out for lunch or drinks after work, they never took Terri's car. She told them that Michael would check the odometer.

Suzanne sometimes invited Terri to do something, and she would reply, "I can't go out. He's checking the mileage on the stupid car again."

"She was under his thumb," Suzanne remembers. "She kept a lot of things under wraps because she was embarrassed to be living this way." Suzanne also thinks that Terri didn't tell her everything because Suzanne was not as submissive as her older sister. "If I had known about a lot of these things, I would not have held back," she told me.

Michael did not get along with Terri's friends, and several of them later accused him of cutting her off from them. Diane Meyer recalls how whenever she would call Terri, Michael would answer the phone and say she wasn't there. She would ask him to leave a message. After months of not hearing from Terri, Diane looked forward to Christmas, when their two families always got together. That Christmas, when Terri saw Diane, she said, "You never call me, you never leave messages." Michael apparently hadn't given her any of Diane's messages.

Diane and Terri stopped seeing each other when Michael claimed that Diane's family had been rude to him at a funeral. When Diane saw Terri at Bobby's college graduation (Bobby had graduated in the same class as Diane), she tried to go over and talk, but Michael physically prevented her.

> *"He has a habit of pulling himself up to his full height in order to intimidate people."*
>
> —DIANE MEYER

Diane Meyer told me how Michael had cut everyone else out of Terri's life. "The only people he couldn't get rid of was her family, because Terri never would have let that happen."

Sue Cobb Pickwell remembers the same thing happening between her and Terri, shortly after she married Michael. Whenever she called Terri to do something, Terri had something planned with Michael.

Diane Meyer remembers seeing Michael "shoot Terri a look" whenever he disapproved of something, and she would shut up. She noticed this occuring more frequently after they got married.

Just prior to her collapse, Terri was beginning to come into her own. If she had blossomed after losing the weight, now she was beginning to realize how beautiful she was. One time Bobby was in his car, waiting at a red light, when a beautiful girl pulled up alongside him. At first, he didn't realize it was his own sister.

> "Terri was attractive to the point she was noticed. She was becoming more who she was the longer that I knew her."
>
> —TERRI WELCH

> "Men noticed her. She was beautiful. She had a witty, funny sense of humor."
>
> —MARIANNE NICHOLSON

When Terri was invited to work-related social functions, she brought her brother, Bobby, because Michael didn't like the people she worked with. When Terri did go out with friends or visited her family, she often worried that she had to be home at a certain time, even when Michael was working.

> "Michael wouldn't let Terri do anything. He had to know where Terri was and who she was with. He was a control freak."
>
> —FRAN CASSLER

"Her mood changed when she went out with us," Bobby said. She enjoyed the attention of other men, but she would stick close to Bobby so they would think she was with him.

Terri was beginning to express unhappiness with her marriage. She flirted with the UPS deliveryman at work and went to lunch with him alone a few times, just prior to her collapse.

> *"Maybe she was realizing that she had made a mistake marrying the first guy who came around."*
>
> —BOBBY SCHINDLER

While Terri was clearly unhappy in her marriage, I couldn't determine whether or not she had actually threatened Michael with a divorce. He has testified that they never discussed divorce. Jackie Rhodes and Bobby Schindler both remember her contemplating divorce.

> *"One of the last times Terri and I were together, she confided to me something that I cannot forget. A few weeks prior to the night Terri collapsed, she and I were talking at the Bennigan's Restaurant in St. Petersburg. Terri asked to speak to me privately, away from Michael, who was with us that evening. We began to talk, and Terri spilled her guts, telling me how absolutely miserable she was, how controlling Michael was, and how horrible their marriage was. I remember like it was yesterday that Terri looked at me and said, 'Bobby I WISH [sic] that I had the guts to divorce Michael, because I can not [sic] take being married with him anymore [sic].' The memory of this conversation is still with me today."*
>
> —BOBBY SCHINDLER, AFFIDAVIT, AUGUST 24, 2003

What if Terri had confronted Michael, and told him she wanted out of the marriage?

VIOLENCE

No one ever witnessed any physical abuse by Michael against Terri. He would often engage in rough "horseplay" that resulted in bruises on her body, but no one ever noticed more serious injuries. The bruises were seen by her entire family, and by Jackie Rhodes, who described them as being the size and shape of fingerprints on her upper arms and thighs. When asked her how she got the bruises, Terri would say, "Michael and I were horsing around." She had never been known to roughhouse prior to being with Michael, and was somewhat fragile physically.

Suzanne recalls that Michael would often pinch and wrestle with her. Whatever Michael's intentions were, when he rough-housed with Suzanne, it caused her pain, and even brought her to tears. Suzanne told me that Terri didn't fight back, or complain. When Suzanne mentioned Michael's bullying to her, Terri would shrug it off.

Suzanne and her family claim that she experienced Michael's temper about a year after Terri's collapse. Michael was living with the Schindlers at the time, and Suzanne had complained about the way Michael treated her parents.

> "Michael started to lunge toward me and I thought that he was going to punch me in the face. . . . My father had to step between us before he got to me. . . . My parents and I were very disturbed and I was extremely frightened, not ever having experienced that side of him. My father phoned his doctor after that and reported the incident to him. Michael was seeing a psychiatrist at the time. His doctor told my father that the next time he has that type of episode to call the police. From that day on, my father had me sleep with my bedroom door locked and a hammer under my pillow. Shortly thereafter, I moved out,

*anxious and not wanting to ever experience Michael's extreme
temper again."*

—SUZANNE VITADAMO

At the time, Michael was seeing a doctor for depression and suicidal thoughts. The fact that Michael's own doctor would tell
Robert Schindler to call the police the next time something like
that happened seems to me to be a pretty clear indication that,
short of violating the doctor–patient privilege, the doctor wanted
to warn them of Michael's potential for violence.

In his deposition in the medical malpractice suit, Michael
stated his doctor prescribed Wellbutrin, Pamelor, Elavil, and Prozac
for his depression, but he said "I never took the medication." Later
he stated that the doctor changed the medication so often because
it made him "sick to my stomach" and "was clouding my thoughts."
He then admitted to taking "one or two pills, three maybe, never
took the whole prescription."

Bobby Schindler claims to have had a similar encounter (which
was corroborated to me by his girlfriend at the time) back when
Michael and Terri were still dating. He remembers getting into a
very heated disagreement with Michael—the details of which he
no longer recalls. Bobby, Michael, Terri, and Bobby's girlfriend at
the time were in the family room of the Schindlers' house in
Pennsylvania.

> *"I remember distinctly that Michael got so upset that he suddenly
> snapped, and grabbed me by the throat and threw me down on
> the couch, had one hand around my neck and the other was in
> the air ready to punch me in the face. I couldn't move and I
> don't know what would have resulted if it weren't for Terri and
> my girlfriend screaming at him to let me go. In hindsight, this is
> something that I should have taken very seriously, and paid*

*more attention to, but I remember that Terri asked me please
not tell our parents because it would upset them too much."*

—BOBBY SCHINDLER

According to Mary, Michael and Scott once had a physical fight
in the Schindlers' kitchen. Michael put Scott in a carotid choke
hold, but Scott was able to get out of it, and the two wrestled on
the floor. When I asked Scott Schiavo about the incident, he was
vague, if not evasive, sticking to generalities by saying that all five
brothers were "very aggressive," but Michael was the least violent.
"Mike was the baby of the family," Scott said, "we used to joke
that he was breast-fed until the age of eighteen."

Scott Schiavo said that the Schindler family "probably made
up" the claims of Michael attacking Bobby and Suzanne.

Diane Meyer had been Terri's friend since childhood, but she
hadn't seen much of her after she married Michael. When she
heard some of the things Terri had said to her friends and family,
Diane told me, "A lightbulb went off in my head." Diane works as
a child-welfare social worker and often performs domestic-abuse
investigations. "These were the remarks that you hear from a
woman who has domestic violence in her history."

CHAPTER EIGHT

"In Sickness and in Health"

The long and bitter conflict between the Schindlers and Michael Schiavo could fill several books. And it probably will. My interest lies only in considering Michael Schiavo's actions and behavior after February 25, 1990, to see if they are consistent with possible criminality. If this is not a balanced portrayal of Michael's life following Terri's collapse, at least it is factual. When you investigate a suspect, it doesn't matter if his mother loved him or he was kind to the old lady next door. You look for behavior that might fit a criminal profile, show motive for a crime, or indicate consciousness of guilt.

GUARDIANSHIP

Michael Schiavo was his wife's legal guardian, which gave him the power to make decisions regarding her treatment. It also gave him control over her estate and her medical and financial records, and allowed him to lay down conditions at the health care facilities where she stayed, including who could visit her and when.

While it was logical that Michael be Terri's guardian, the control that he exerted over even the smallest details concerning her treatment, the efforts that he made to restrict access to her medical records and permission to visit her, and finally the stubbornness with which he pursued her legally sanctioned death are extreme to the point of suspicion. At the very least, they demonstrate a mania for control that borders on the pathological.

As early as July 16, 1993, the Schindler family told Michael in a letter (they were no longer speaking) that they were willing to assume full responsibility for Terri. In the days leading up to the final removal of her feeding tube, they offered Michael as much as $1 million to surrender the guardianship and allow them to care for Terri. Once her feeding tube was removed, they asked him to allow her to die at their home.

Michael Schiavo refused to give up any control over his wife. In fact, his control only increased as the legal battle between him and the Schindlers continued, until, toward the end of Terri's life, family members had to pass police barricades and be physically searched prior to visiting Terri on her deathbed—when Michael permitted them to do so.

Starting in early 1993, Michael refused to keep the Schindlers informed about Terri's condition. On several occasions they did not know that Terri had been hospitalized and almost died. Not only did Michael not keep them posted about Terri's condition, but he told caregivers specifically not to inform her parents. On several occasions he denied them visiting privileges and refused to let them see Terri's medical records until ordered by the court to do so.

The secretive and controlling nature of his guardianship over Terri began almost immediately after her collapse. In Humana Hospital during the first days following the incident, Robert Schindler spoke with Daniel Greico, Michael Schiavo's boss at Agostino's, who also happened to be an attorney. Greico asked him to sign some documents allowing Michael to be appointed official guardian with control over Terri's medical care. Greico said this would expedite any emergency treatment.

Robert signed the papers, thinking this was the best thing for his daughter. In the fifteen years that followed, he has never seen the guardianship papers. Whether or not Robert signed papers doesn't really matter, since on June 18, 1990, Michael Schiavo was appointed Terri's legal guardian at a hearing in the circuit court, Sixth Judicial District, Florida Probate Division (St. Petersburg), following an investigation that determined her to be incapacitated. In court documents filed May 21, 1990, Michael Schiavo stated that the Schindlers had no objections to him being appointed guardian. The Schindlers did not appear at the hearing, and say Michael never mentioned it to them, even though at the time they were in daily contact. They were not aware of the investigation declaring Terri incapacitated. None of this information was disclosed to them until they conducted their own investigation in June 2004, when they found the court files.

As Terri's legal guardian, Michael was able to control all of her medical records and information concerning her treatment. On several occasions, the Schindlers were not informed of hospitalizations or diagnostic procedures performed on their daughter. This is why, for example, they did not learn of the bone scan until more than ten years after it had been conducted. Many of Terri's medical records are no longer available, and the only copies appear to be in Michael's possession.

Several months after Terri's collapse, the Schindlers rented a home, which they put in Michael's name, because they were going through bankruptcy proceedings. Michael moved in with them. In September 1990, they brought Terri home to live with them, yet three weeks later returned her to College Park skilled care and rehabilitation facility because they were overwhelmed by her care needs.

For first two years following Terri's collapse, Michael Schiavo was, by all accounts, completely devoted to her. He quit his job and visited Terri almost every day, usually with Mary Schindler. He paid close attention to the details of her care and therapy.

"He was very doting in the beginning. He was more respectful to her after she collapsed. Her hair and makeup had to be done. I thought it was great at the time."

—SUZANNE VITADAMO

Michael and the Schindlers both worked very hard for "Terri Schiavo Day" at St. Petersburg Beach, raising approximately $50,000 to help Terri get experimental thalamic stimulator implants put in her brain, meant to stimulate brain activity and hopefully improve her condition. Prudential employees also undertook their own fund-raising efforts, over objections by management. In December 1990, Michael took Terri to California to have the implants put in. Mary could not go with them because her own mother was sick. Michael got angry with her because he felt that she had dumped all the responsibility in his lap. He called Mary from California, complaining that he was lonely and having difficulty dealing with Terri.

The implants required further therapy, and one doctor suggested Terri go to Shands Medical Center in Gainesville, Florida. Michael and the Schindlers often talked about sending Terri to Shands, but they were waiting for the medical malpractice case to be resolved in the hope of having the necessary funds.

Terri had become Michael's full-time job. Prudential paid Terri's salary for a year. Life and medical insurance were provided as part of Terri's employee benefit package. She would receive her salary until the middle of 1992. At that time, she began to receive Social Security payments. Michael lived off these funds.

Q. What did you do with your wife's jewelry?

A. My wife's jewelry?

Q. Yeah.

A. Um, I think I took her engagement ring and her . . . what do they call it . . . diamond wedding band and I made a ring for myself.

—MICHAEL SCHIAVO, DEPOSITION IN GUARDIANSHIP

CASE, NOVEMBER 19, 1993

Whether this was a symbolic act in order to end the marriage short of divorce (which would have lost him Terri's estate) or Michael simply wanted some jewelry for himself, it demonstrates that by the summer of 1993, Michael did not expect Terri to recover.

In the same deposition, Michael admitted to cashing Terri's $10,000 life-insurance living-needs benefit and putting the money in a safe-deposit box. In 1992, he had Terri's cats put to sleep, "on the advice of my mother-in-law." Mary Schindler disputes this, saying that Michael wanted to get rid of the cats because he was living with a girlfriend who had a dog. He asked if the Schindlers could take the cats, but they couldn't because Bobby was allergic.

Terri had been devoted to those cats. She had found the first one, Shanna, by the side of the road, nearly dead from starvation. She took it to a vet, who told her the cat would not live. Instead of euthanizing the cat, Terri took it home and nursed it back to health. Then she got another cat, which she named Tolly, because she feared that Shanna was lonely.

Michael moved out of the Schindlers' house in May 1992. At this point he had been dating Cindy Brashers Shook since January. The Schindlers had encouraged Michael to see other women. Suzanne's ex-husband Danny Carr arranged a weekend at a resort hotel for Michael and Cindy.

If the Schindlers wanted Michael to get on with his life, they didn't expect him to drop out of sight. When he hooked up with Cindy, the Schindlers saw Michael much less frequently. Mary, who didn't drive, no longer had a ride to the hospital. Michael would still visit Terri regularly, but Mary would have to call him to get a ride.

Cindy told a local radio audience on April 25, 2001, that she was the first girl to go out with Michael after Terri's collapse and "I dated him for a year." In a deposition taken on May 8 of that year, Cindy characterized her relationship with Michael this way: "We were not romantically involved." According to Cindy, they only "dated" once—the first time they ever went out, then after that they were "best friends."

Whatever Cindy meant by "dating" and "best friends," it's clear that she and Michael did have some kind of relationship. On the day that the medical malpractice award was announced, Michael and Cindy decided they should end their relationship. Cindy later described the breakup as civil. In that same deposition, she said that Michael's behavior around that time worried her. From Cindy's own statements, it's clear that Michael didn't let go so easily.

According to Cindy's deposition testimony, a couple of months after they broke up, Michael got a job as an orderly in the hospital where Cindy worked and often came to her floor looking for her. Cindy testified that Michael was eventually fired from that job, although Cindy said that she didn't think it was as a result of her complaints to supervisors about his behavior. She called what Michael did to her "stalking." Cindy also testified that on approximately ten separate occasions while she was driving, she would look up in her rearview mirror and see Michael right behind her. When she changed lanes, he would follow her.

> One time when he was behind me in traffic. He got next to me in a two-lane going the same way, and he changed lanes basically right on top of where I was at, and I had to swerve not to be hit. I had to swerve off the road. Michael ran me off the road.
> —CINDY SHOOK, DEPOSITION, MAY 8, 2001

Cindy characterized Michael's behavior as "stalking, dangerous," and "potentially life-threatening."

Once Cindy married Donald Shook, someone called their home and left long, silent phone messages over a period of about a year. On some days they received twelve to fifteen calls, to the point where the message machine would run out of tape.

After her appearance on the radio show, both Bobby Schindler and Schindler family private investigator Kim Takacs spoke to Cindy and then signed sworn affidavits recounting their conversations with her. They were interested in finding out anything Michael might have said to Cindy regarding Terri's end-of-life wishes. One thing they both noted was that eight and a half years after their breakup, Cindy still seemed afraid of Michael.

In her deposition, Cindy characterized Michael as "unstable." While she claimed he had never been violent, she expressed concern "about retaliation because I have a child—I have children and a husband."

At the same time that he was going out with Cindy Shook, Michael also developed a relationship with Trudy Capone, a registered nurse who was caring for Terri at Sabel Palms, a nursing home. When I called Trudy, she was at first reluctant to speak to me, saying that "Terri is dead and nothing will bring her back." I told her I wanted to know about her relationship with Michael. She said that while she hadn't been romantically involved with him, they saw each other frequently. When she first met Michael, he was very nice and complimentary, but later he went out of his way to humiliate and embarrass her, particularly in front of other people.

"Michael is evil, evil, evil. There is no other word for him. Everything that is around Michael turns bad. Once you get to know the real Michael, you wanted to run, but he would chase

you. He is so controlling that he needs to know where you are and who you are talking to all the time."

—TRUDY CAPONE

Trudy considered herself lucky that she didn't get too involved with Michael Schiavo. He tried to get sympathy, often complaining about his situation. Trudy nearly fell for it.

"Michael went crazy on me when I ended our friendship because he was calling me so much and I needed space," Trudy said. She described how Michael got a job where she worked and sent her roses.

The relationships that both Trudy Capone and Cindy Shook had with Michael Schiavo ended on November 10, 1992—the day the medical malpractice award was announced.

During the medical malpractice trial, the plaintiffs presented evidence by Dr. David Baras, chief of rehabilitation at Bayfront Medical Center, and Lawrence Foreman, a rehabilitation specialist, who testified that Terri would have a normal life span and would need extensive and expensive rehabilitation care throughout her life. Michael said he wanted to become a nurse so he could take Terri home and care for her there. That was one of the reasons the plaintiffs' attorneys were asking for $20 million.

"I believe in the vows that I took with my wife. Through sickness, in health, for richer or poorer. I married my wife because I love her and I want to spend the rest of my life with her. I'm going to do that."

—MICHAEL SCHIAVO, MEDICAL MALPRACTICE
TESTIMONY, NOVEMBER 5, 1992

A few weeks after the verdict, Robert Schindler saw Michael at the nursing home during a visit to Terri. He asked Michael about the settlement.

"We'll talk about it another time," Michael said.

Michael got the check in December. The Schindlers didn't see him again until Valentine's Day, 1993.

The Schindlers and Michael disagree about what happened next, although everyone agrees there was a loud argument and they never spoke again.

HERE IS ROBERT AND MARY SCHINDLER'S VERSION OF EVENTS

They walked into Terri's room and Michael was there, studying his nursing books.

"I approached him because the money had come in and she was still in a nursing home," Robert says. "I wanted her in a rehab hospital. She was showing signs of improvement. The University of Florida had a state-of-the-art rehab center. The doctor wanted testing done on her there."

Robert asked Michael when Terri was going to get the therapy he had promised when they were talking about how to spend the malpractice award money.

"Terri is my wife," Michael said. "I make all the decisions."

Michael threw a tantrum. He threw his books across the room. He went after Robert, but Mary got in between them.

"We almost had a fight," Bob says. "There was fire in his eyes. He was outraged."

"You have nothing to say about this," Michael said, going to the door. "You're never going to see her again. I'm going to see my attorney."

HERE IS WHAT MICHAEL TOLD LARRY KING
ON OCTOBER 27, 2003

KING: OK, the break with the family.

SCHIAVO: Her father and mother came into the room. And they closed the door. And they asked the big question, How much money am I going to get? And I told them I wasn't going to get any money.

KING: Out of the malpractice?

SCHIAVO: Out of the malpractice suit. Then he argued with me for a little while. And then he pointed at Terri in the wheelchair and says, How much am I going to get from her money?

And I said, you have to go talk to the courts about that.

KING: She got money, too?

SCHIAVO: Yes, Terri got money.

KING: OK.

FELOS: Terri got the bulk of the money.

KING: OK, which was used for her rehab and for her medical expenses?

FELOS: Medical expenses.

SCHIAVO: From there, it blew up. He wanted to go out in the hall and have a fistfight. It was crazy. It was ludicrous.

KING: Did this shock you?

SCHIAVO: No, because he's always wanted the money. He always wanted money out of this. He even testified in the first trial that he was angry that he didn't get any money.

KING: And what about her mom?

SCHIAVO: Her mom kind of just stood between us. She yelled at me not to do this, don't do this. They stormed out of the nursing home. And from then, they tried to sue me numerous times to have me removed as guardian. And from then, they really basically didn't have any care with Terri. They hardly showed up to see Terri. Their main concern to me was the father was angry because he didn't get any money.

KING: So what do you make of what they say about you? I mean, are you shocked?

SCHIAVO: No. I wouldn't expect any less from Mr. Schindler.

Shortly after the Valentine's Day fight, Michael Schiavo instructed the staff at the nursing home not to provide information about Terri's medical condition to anyone but himself or the doctor. He also posted a "do not rescusitate" order in her medical file.

In August 1993, the Schindlers were not told when Terri was hospitalized for a urinary-tract infection that had developed into sepsis. And they weren't informed that Michael had asked the medical staff not to give her antibiotics for the infection. If left untreated, the sepsis could have killed Terri. And Michael knew it.

Q. And did he tell you what would occur if you failed to treat that infection? What did he tell you?

A. That sometimes urinary tract infection will turn to sepsis.

Q. And sepsis is what?

A. An infection throughout the body.

Q. And what would be the result of untreated sepsis be to the patient?

A. The patient would pass on.

Q. So when you made the decision not to treat Terri's bladder infection you, in effect, were making a decision to allow her to pass on?

A. I was making a decision on what Terri would want.

Q. Did you instruct the doctor not to treat the bladder infection?

A. Uh-huh. Yes.

—MICHAEL SCHIAVO, DEPOSITION IN GUARDIANSHIP
CASE, NOVEMBER 19, 1993

The staff at Sabel Palms nursing home told Michael that Florida state law prohibited them from denying lifesaving treatment to Terri.

Q. You did change your decision not to treat the bladder condition, correct?

A. I had to change my decision.

. . .

Q. Why have you changed your opinion?

A. Because evidently there is a law out there that says I can't do it.

—MICHAEL SCHIAVO, DEPOSITION IN GUARDIANSHIP
CASE, NOVEMBER 19, 1993

When the Schindlers found out that Michael was trying to end Terri's life, they made their first effort to have him legally removed as guardian. This attempt, like every other challenge to Michael's guardianship, was unsuccessful. John Pecarek was appointed guardian ad litem (someone named by a court to manage the interests of an incapacitated person) to investigate the case and offer suggestions to the court. Pecarek found that Michael had acted appropriately and attentively toward Terri. Reports that Michael had brought nurses to tears by berating them for failing to adequately take care of his wife were used as evidence of his devotion.

"Although I have concluded that Mr. Schiavo is a nursing home administrator's nightmare, I believe the ward gets more care and

attention as a result of Mr. Schiavo's advocacy and complaining on her behalf."

—JOHN PECAREK, GUARDIAN AD LITEM REPORT,

MARCH 1, 1994

This report was filed after Michael had already told doctors not to treat Terri's urinary-tract infection, which he knew would have resulted in her death.

Clearly, something had changed. While Michael remained very involved in Terri's care, it's obvious to me that it was no longer with the goal of getting her better. And by August 1993, he was already trying to end her life.

The medical malpractice award was the turning point, not only in his relations with the Schindlers but also in his attitude toward Terri. During his November 19, 1993, guardianship case deposition, Michael described how when the attorneys were talking about a $20 million award, he and the Schindlers discussed spending the money on Terri's care at home. "And then the case went bust and belly up," Michael said. "There were no commitments. . . . And it kind of, like, faded away."

Years later, Fran Cassler told investigators that shortly after the medical malpractice verdict, everyone had gone out to dinner to celebrate. At the dinner, Michael's mother, Claire, who is now dead, pulled Fran aside and said: "Don't tell the Schindlers, but there is going to be trouble. I know my son and he's going to renege on his promise to take care of Terri."

After the medical malpractice award came in, "Michael started the methodical process of trying to kill Terri," according to Fran.

CHAPTER NINE

"Till Death Do Us Part"

From 1993 until her death in 2005, Michael denied Terri any form of therapy. Even after Michael Schiavo had denied Terri therapy for years, several nurses reported her trying to speak, even saying certain words like "mommy," "help," and "pain." The Schindlers always claimed that she communicated with them, particularly her mother, Mary. While the Schindlers claim they saw improvements in her ability to swallow, talk, and respond to others, Michael consistently argued that all forms of therapy were ineffective. He stated that he had already tried everything possible, but nothing would restore any of Terri's functioning. This is a matter of medical dispute, as doctors hired by both sides have argued that she would or would not have benefited from therapy. The fact that Michael had control over her medical decisions meant that she wouldn't get any.

The initial guardianship plan, filed by Daniel Greico on September 5, 1990, stated that physical, occupational, and speech therapies for Terri were "not useful at this time." After this, Terri did receive therapy, including the experimental thalamic stimulator implant in her brain. Yet this was all prior to the malpractice award. After that, Michael kept her in nursing homes, severely restricting not only her therapy but also stimulation. He didn't let her listen to music or go outside. He ordered the shades in her room to be always kept closed.

He also started making plans for her death.

> *"The preceding day I had learned that a local funeral home*
> *has had an open file for Terri's funeral since 1993, opened*
> *by Michael Schiavo. When I went to the funeral home to*
> *investigate, I asked the funeral director if I could see the file. He*
> *left the room to ask if he could show it to me. When he came*
> *back he said he had gotten in trouble for even revealing the file's*
> *existence."*
>
> —BOBBY SCHINDLER, SEPTEMBER 4, 2003, AFFIDAVIT

When it was first suggested to Michael that Terri's feeding tube be removed, he was opposed to the idea.

Q. Was it Doctor Harrison's suggestion the feeding tube be removed?

A. It wasn't a suggestion, it was just talk. He just mentioned it.

Q. How did he mention it? What did he say?

A. He was talking about removing the feeding tubes, and I said I couldn't do that to Terri.

> —MICHAEL SCHIAVO, DEPOSITION, NOVEMBER 11 1993

Michael's mother, Claire, died in 1997. In the obituary, her survivors included "Michael and his fiancée Jodi." This was the first time the Schindlers heard that Michael was planning to get married. Yet he refused to divorce Terri.

On March 5, 1997, Michael hired George Felos, a Florida attorney specializing in right-to-die cases. Papers Michael signed gave Felos the authority "to represent him in connection with the withdrawal and/or refusal of medical treatments." Terri's medical fund would pay Felos's legal fees. One of the first thing Felos did was have the finances sealed; however, records show that Felos has been paid $380,000 out of Terri's estate. Much of this was for legal work Felos performed trying to get Terri's feeding tube removed.

Felos had represented the family of Estelle Browning, an eighty-six-year-old woman who had suffered a stroke and remained unresponsive. Although she had left a living will stating that she did not wish to be kept alive artificially, state law at the time prohibited the removal of nourishment and hydration when death was not imminent. In 1989, Browning died of natural causes while the case was still in litigation, yet the Florida Supreme Court eventually ruled that a living will could permit the withholding of nourishment and hydration even when death was not imminent.

In his book, *Litigation as Spiritual Practice*, Felos describes visiting Browning at her nursing home.

As Mrs. Browning lay motionless before my gaze, I suddenly heard a loud, deep moan and scream and wondered if the nursing home personnel heard it and would respond to the unfortunate resident. In the next moment, as this cry of pain and torment continued, I realized it was Mrs. Browning.

I felt the mid-section of my body open and noticed a strange quality to the light in the room. I sensed her soul in agony. As she screamed I heard her say, in confusion, "Why am I still here . . . why am I here?" My soul touched hers and in some way I communicated that she was still locked in her body. I promised I would do everything in my power to gain the release her soul cried for. With that the screaming immediately stopped. I felt like I was back in my head again, the room resumed its normal appearance, and Mrs. Browning, as she had throughout this experience, lay silent.

On May 8, 1998, Felos sent the Schindlers formal notice of a petition for authorization to discontinue artificial life support. The petition stated, "Discontinuance of artificial life support is not only in accordance with the Ward's intent, it is in the best interests of the Ward." In this case, the ward is Terri Schiavo. The petition acknowledged that Terri's estate at the time was in excess of $500,000, which Michael would inherit as intestate heir if she died while they were still married.

Since Michael was no longer communicating with the Schindlers, except through the courts, Michael's lawyer Deborah Bushnell asked the court to sign another order that would be sent on to the Schindlers in order to inform them that her client was attempting to end their daughter's life.

> "Attorney Felos, the guardian, and I feel that the receipt of a petition for payment of attorney fees regarding this issue would not be the best and kindest way for the ward's parents to learn that this issue [removal of feeding tube] is being considered."
> —DEBORAH BUSHNELL TO JUDGE MARK SHAMES,
> MAY 6, 1997

At the time, it was not legal in Florida to remove the feeding tube of a patient who had not made an advance directive and was not terminally ill. Over the next couple years, the Florida legislature was lobbied by several individuals, many of them associated with the hospice where Terri was eventually admitted, and George Felos, to change the requirement that a patient be "terminally ill" before life-prolonging procedures can be withdrawn. In 1999, the law was revised to redefine "terminally ill" patient and allow for the removal of nutrition and hydration from a patient in a "persistent vegetative state" who had not left advance directives.

Whether or not the law was changed to specifically include Terri Schiavo, as some claim, it certainly applied to her case, at least if medical experts determined that Terri was in a "persistent vegetative state."

Felos asked for a guardian ad litem to be appointed, in order to investigate the case and make suggestions to the court. The second guardian ad litem, Richard Pearse, submitted his report on December 20, 1998. He found that the only evidence supporting Michael's claim that Terri would have wanted her feeding tube removed was Michael's own statements, and he had never before mentioned conversations he reported having with her on the subject. Pearse went on to say that Michael's "credibility is necessarily adversely affected by the obvious financial benefit to him of being the ward's sole heir." Reviewing the financial records, Pearse valued Terri's estate at more than $750,000.

> "Mr. Schiavo's credibility is also adversely affected by the chronology of this case. For the first four years (approximately) following the ward's accident, he aggressively pursued every manner of treatment and rehabilitation conceivable, as well as lawsuits to compensate the ward for her injuries with which he presumably argued that she would require substantial funds for future care and treatment. At or around the time the litigation was finally concluded, he has a change of heart concerning further treatment which lead [sic], according to the ward's parents, to his falling out with them. From that point forward, the ward's husband has isolated the ward from her parents, has on at least one occasion refused to consent for the ward to be treated for an infection, and ultimately, four years later, has filed the instant petition for the withdrawal of life support on the basis of evidence apparently known only to him which could have been asserted at any time during the ward's illness."
>
> —RICHARD PEARSE, GUARDIAN AD LITEM REPORT,
> DECEMBER 20, 1998

The legal struggle over guardianship went to trial on January 24, 2000, in front of Pinellas-Pasco county circuit court judge George Greer. George Felos elicited testimony from Michael, Scott, and Joan Schiavo, Michael's sister-in-law, that Terri had made statements indicating she would not have wanted to be kept alive if incapacitated. On cross-examination, both Scott and Joan Schiavo admitted that they hadn't talked about these conversations with anyone prior to recounting them to George Felos.

On February 11, Judge Greer ruled that Michael was authorized to remove Terri's feeding tube.

> *"The court does find that Terri Schiavo did make statements*
> *which are credible and reliable with regard to her intention."*
> —JUDGE GEORGE GREER, FEBRUARY 11, 2000

During the trial, the Schindlers had testified to Terri's being Roman Catholic, and the fact that she had gone to great lengths to save the lives of animals. Despite seeing family members who had been crippled and incapacitated, Terri never mentioned to them any wishes that she would not be kept alive in such a state.

Terri's friend Diane Meyer told me that she remembered talking with her about Karen Ann Quinlan, a twenty-one-year-old woman from New Jersey who had fallen into a coma due to alcohol and drug abuse. Diane repeated a joke that had gone around at the time: "What's the state vegetable of New Jersey? Karen Ann Quinlan." It was the first time in their friendship that Diane saw Terri lose her temper. She said she didn't approve of Quinlan's parents removing her life support.

"Where there is life," Terri said, "there is hope."

Diane clearly remembers the conversation, which occurred years after Karen Ann Quinlan had been taken off life support and died, even recalling what Terri wore that day.

"Life was too precious a gift for her," Diane told me. "It was something she respected too much."

Fran Cassler told investigators about a 1991 conversation she overheard between Michael and a friend of hers during a concert on the beach. "He was talking to anyone who would listen to him and feel sorry for him." According to Fran, he said: "How should I know what Terri wanted?"

Fran's friend Sherry Payne recalled the same conversation: "We were all sitting on blankets. . . . Michael said he had no idea what Terri would want to do in the condition she is in. He said he did not know."

These comments are similar in sense and wording to statements that Bobby Schindler and Kim Takacs, a private investigator working for the Schindlers, swore that Cindy Brashers Shook made to them concerning Michael's conversations with her. In her deposition, Cindy said that in their affidavits, Bobby and Kim had misrepresented what she told them. Cindy stated that Michael had said: "How the hell should I know? We were young. We never spoke of this." She understood his statements to mean he didn't know what to do with Terri at that time in terms of her treatment and his getting on with his own life, not that he didn't know what her end-of-life wishes might have been. In her deposition Cindy specifically said that Michael never mentioned anything about Terri's end-of-life wishes to her. Cindy is making a distinction that is lost on me. If Michael said he didn't know what to do about Terri's treatment and his own life, it's not unreasonable to understand that to mean that Terri had not discussed such issues with him. And since Cindy said that Michael never mentioned Terri's wishes that he later testified to, this would indicate that he forgot or did not mention his conversations with Terri that he so clearly remembered during the guardianship trial. In a sworn affidavit, Trudy Capone corroborated Cindy's original statement that Michael said he didn't know what Terri would have wanted.

> *"He never knew what Terri wanted. He would confide in me all the time about how he did not know, and he would ask me what I thought he should do."*
> —TRUDY CAPONE, AFFIDAVIT, MAY 9, 2001

Collectively, these statements are as powerful as the evidence presented in Judge Greer's court that Terri had allegedly told her husband and in-laws that she would have wanted artificial life support removed.

In April 2000, Terri was transferred to Hospice of the Florida Suncoast. In order to be admitted to hospice, the patient has to be "terminally ill" and certified by two physicians to have six months or less to live. Terri was examined and certified to be terminally ill by Dr. Victor Gambone and Dr. William Moore on April 11, 2000. She was said to be in a "permanent vegetative state," which is not a recognized terminal condition under federally mandated hospice guidelines.

George Felos had been on the hospice board of directors and also served as chairman. Records filed with the Florida secretary of state show that Felos was still listed as director of the hospice in May 2000.

Following a year of legal appeals, Terri's feeding tube was removed for the first time on April 24, 2001. The next day, Cindy Brashers Shook called in to a local radio show and spoke on air with the DJ about her yearlong relationship with Michael Schiavo. After hearing a tape of the broadcast, and having both Bobby Schindler and private investigator Kim Takacs speak to Cindy and then swear out affidavits describing their conversations, the Schindlers filed an emergency motion with Judge Greer using Cindy's statements that

Michael did not know Terri's end-of-life wishes as evidence that he had lied in testimony on this crucial issue.

Judge Greer dismissed the motion as untimely, saying that it was too late to introduce new evidence. The Schindlers filed a civil suit claiming that Michael had perjured himself. Pending this new trial, Terri's feeding tube was reinserted on April 26.

Michael filed an emergency petition to have the tube removed again. That and the civil suit, which never went to trial, generated another series of legal battles.

In October 2002, Michael petitioned Judge Greer to have Terri's body cremated after her death, arguing that Terri had always been afraid of bugs and would not want to be buried. Greer granted the request.

A month later, the Schindlers submitted evidence, including the bone scan, indicating Terri's collapse might have been caused by possible abuse.

> "The court concludes that while it might be interesting to pursue the issue of trauma as it may have occurred almost twelve years ago, that has nothing to do with Theresa Marie Schiavo in 2002 and the Mandate of the Second District Court of Appeal."
> —JUDGE GEORGE GREER, NOVEMBER 22, 2002

But the issue of abuse was far from over. If the bone scan does not show clear evidence of domestic violence, the Schindlers and their legal team were able to document other troubling charges against Michael concerning his treatment of Terri after her collapse.

Carla Iyer worked as a registered nurse at Palm Gardens Convalescent Center from April 1995 to July 1996.

When I spoke to Carla, she said that Michael would not allow Terri any form of stimulation. Once, when she tried to put a

washcloth in Terri's hand to keep her fingers from curling together, Michael told her to take it out, because that was therapy.

Q. Are you aware of any treatment anywhere that can help Terri?

A. There is no treatment anywhere that can help Terri. No.

Q. If there were, what would you do?

A. I would be there in a heartbeat.

—MICHAEL SCHIAVO, TESTIMONY IN GUARDIANSHIP

TRIAL, JANUARY 24, 2000

Iyer describes Michael bullying the staff at Palm Garden. "The
atmosphere throughout the facility was dominated by Mr. Schiavo's intimidation." Michael would say, "This is my order and
you're going to follow it." He had an "overbearing attitude" and
used "menacing body language."

When I spoke with Carla, she confirmed everything in her affidavit. She said that Michael would not allow Terri any form of
stimulation. There were no pictures or decorations in her room. If
he found flowers in her room, he threw them away. The blinds were
to be kept closed at all times. She was never allowed to leave her
room, although Iyer and other nurses would take her to the nurses'
station while someone stayed guard outside in case Michael arrived.

Michael was adamant that the Schindlers not be informed
about Terri's condition. (A 1996 court order required Michael to
provide the Schindlers with medical records and allowed caregivers to inform them of Terri's condition.) At Palm Gardens, the
nursing home where Terri stayed from 1994 to 2000, a sign was
posted on her bed stating that under no circumstances was her

family to be contacted. Her chart also included Michael's instructions that Terri not be treated by nurses who were minorities or males, saying that he didn't want them to see her naked. He wanted the nurses around Terri to be females, preferably blondes. Similar orders had been made at Sabel Palms.

Heidi Law worked at Palm Gardens after Carla Iyer, and corroborates her statements that Terri received no therapy on Michael's orders. Staff told her, "Do what Michael told you or you will lose your job." She also stated that when Terri got sick, "Michael's mood would improve."

In both Sabel Palms and Palm Gardens, Michael would lock himself in the room when he visited Terri and remain there for some twenty minutes.

"We were convinced that he was abusing her, and probably saying cruel, terrible things to her because she would be so upset when he left."

—HEIDI LAW, AFFIDAVIT, SEPTEMBER 1, 2003

Terri's feeding tube was removed for the second time on October 15, 2003. Six days later, the Florida state legislature passed "Terri's Law," which gave Governor Jeb Bush the power to issue a "one-time stay in certain cases." Bush immediately issued an executive order to reinsert Terri's feeding tube and ordered that a guardian ad litem be appointed to review the case.

"I never wanted Terri to die. I still don't. I was so frustrated that I could not help Terri. I am sure that I was sometimes unkind to the aides—even shouted at them. This was not because I wanted Terri dead, but because I desperately wanted her alive. I blamed myself because I could not bring her back."

—MICHAEL SCHIAVO, OCTOBER 20, 2003

The third guardian ad litem, Jay Wolfson, submitted his report on December 1, 2003. Wolfson concluded that Terri was in a persistent vegetative state with no chance of improvement.

Terri's Law was eventually ruled unconstitutional, and the legal issues were thrown back to Judge Greer's court, eventually resulting in the removal of her feeding tube for the third time on March 18, 2005.

Michael Schiavo would probably say that many of the people I have quoted in the last three chapters are lying. I find this difficult to believe, as different people who never knew one another say the same things about him. It is abundantly clear that as soon as he received the medical malpractice award, Michael Schiavo began a relentless campaign to end Terri's life. While she was alive, her trust was used to pay her medical bills and the legal fees generated by his effort to end her life. Once she died, he would inherit whatever was left. He would be free to marry his girlfriend, with whom he had two children.

Since Terri's collapse, Michael became qualified as an emergency medical technician, a respiratory therapist, and finally a registered nurse.

> "When I heard Michael had become a nurse, I'd go to that hospital like I'd go fishing with Scott Peterson."
>
> —TERRI WELCH, A FRIEND OF
> TERRI SCHIAVO FROM PRUDENTIAL

Three-year-old Terri plays with little brother Bobby, 1966.

Terri with her doll in the Schindler living room.

Terri and Bobby "were like twins."

Terri and Bobby celebrate Christmas 1968.

First communion for Terri, far left, 1972.

Confirmation for Terri, nine, and Bobby, seven.

Terri and Bobby on their confirmation day.

Twelve-year-old Terri with her favorite pet, Bucky, a Labrador retriever.

Terri, Robert, and Suzanne Schindler in front of the fireplace at their Pennsylvania home.

Terri, Bobby, and Suzanne on a Florida vacation in 1978.

Terri and her mother, Mary, at Terri's graduation from Archbishop Wood High School, 1981. She began dieting shortly after graduation.

Robert; his mother,
Katherine; Bobby;
Suzanne; Terri;
and Mary in
1983. Terri has
already lost weight.

Michael Schiavo and Terri
Schindler, December 1983.
They would get married a
year later.

By 1983, Terri was
slimming down.

*Theresa Marie Schindler
on her wedding day,
November 10, 1984.*

The bride and her parents.

*Terri with Suzanne and brother Bobby
at her wedding.*

*Terri and
Michael
exchange
wedding vows.*

Bobby, Suzanne, Terri, and Michael at the Schindler house, Christmas 1984.

The Schindler family at Bobby's graduation from Florida State, 1987.

Suzanne, Bobby, and Terri at Bobby's graduation. Terri now weighed about one hundred and twenty pounds.

Terri, Michael, Bobby, Mary, Bill Winslow, and Suzanne.
Christmas in Florida, 1987.

Terri with her parents in Florida, 1987.

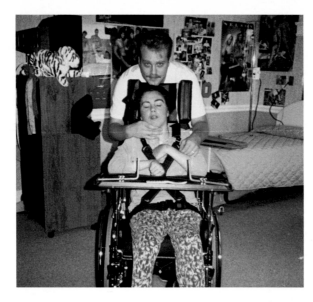

By all accounts, Michael took good care of Terri during the first two years after her collapse.

Michael had the nurses put makeup on Terri and fix her hair.

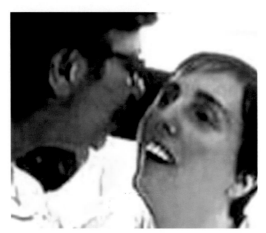

Terri responds to her mother's playful attention.

CHAPTER TEN

Time Doesn't Lie

Timeline is one of the most crucial aspects of an investigation. Events happen at specific times. They occur in sequence and consequence, affected by what has happened previously. While people might be mistaken about their time estimates, there are certain possibilities that can be eliminated because of time and witnesses' knowledge of events as they transpired. Time has its own laws and logical consequences. It is the pattern that makes sense of people's recollections, and often provides the proof that contradicts a suspect's story.

The following description of the events of February 24 to February 25, 1990, is based on interviews of involved parties, official reports, testimony, and court records. Precise times are used whenever possible.

Morning—Terri wakes up and goes to hairdresser.

10:00–10:30 A.M.—Michael described this as the time he usually woke up on Saturday. He stated that he did not see Terri that morning. His testimony is vague as to whether he saw her later that day before going to work.

2:00–3:00 P.M.—Jackie Rhodes calls Terri in the early afternoon and asks about her hair appointment. Terri has been crying. She is very upset because she had a fight with Michael over the eighty dollars she spent on her hair. Jackie offers to come over, but Terri says that she is going to see her brother, Bobby.

Approximately 3:00 P.M.—Terri goes to Bobby's apartment and tells him that she and Michael have been fighting, but doesn't state the reason. Bobby asks Terri to go out with him and his roommate that evening, but she declines, telling Bobby that she is going to church with their parents. Before she leaves, Terri irons the jeans Bobby is planning to wear that night.

4:00–5:00 P.M.—Terri attends Saturday mass at St. John's Church, St. Petersburg, with her mother and father.

5:00 P.M.—Terri, her mother and father have dinner at Fran Cassler's home.

7:00 P.M.—Terri's parents decide to go home. They ask Terri to come with them. In two separate cars, Terri and her parents drive to their house. Terri sits and talks with them for approximately a half hour.

7:30 P.M.—Terri tells her parents she needs to get home and will call once she gets there.

8:00 P.M.—Returning to the Thunder Bay Apartments, Terri visits Bobby, who asks her again if she wants to go out with him and his roommate. Terri says she can't.

Approximately 8:30 P.M.—Terri calls her mother, crying and complaining of pain from the yeast infection they had previously discussed that evening.

Sometime between 11:00 P.M. February 24 and 2:00 A.M. February 25—Michael Schiavo returns home from his job as night manager of Agostino's. He has made several different statements regarding the time he came home that night.

Sometime between 4:30 and 5:00 A.M.—According to his testimony and public statements, Michael is awakened by a *thud* and gets up to find Terri lying unconscious on the floor outside the bathroom.

5:40 A.M.—St. Petersburg Police Department incident sheet lists this as the time when the 911 call came into the fire department. While Michael claims to have called 911 first, Robert Schindler says Michael called him first and he told Michael to call 911.

Approximately 5:45 A.M.—Robert Schindler calls Bobby and tells him to go to Terri's apartment because something has happened to her.

5:50 A.M.—Bobby Schindler arrives at Terri and Michael's apartment. Michael opens the door for him, then goes to living room. Bobby shakes Terri's shoulder and calls her name. She is gasping for breath.

5:52 A.M.—Fire-department paramedics arrive at the apartment and begin resuscitation efforts. Shortly afterward, the SunStar ambulance arrives.

6:11 A.M.—Fire-department paramedics request a police unit for assistance. St. Petersburg police dispatch Officers Brewer and Tower.

6:33 A.M.—Police arrive. They see no signs of struggle and do not observe anything suspicious in the apartment.

6:34 A.M.—After working on Terri for forty-two minutes, the paramedics begin to transport her to Humana Northside Hospital. Michael rides in the ambulance. He has given his keys to police to lock up the apartment.

Approximately 6:30 A.M.—Bobby Schindler calls his father, Robert, and tells them where the ambulance is taking Terri. They leave within ten minutes. It is a twenty-minute drive to the hospital. Bobby drives to the hospital himself.

6:46 A.M.—SunStar ambulance arrives at Humana Northside Hospital with Terri and Michael.

6:59 A.M.—Sunrise on February 25, 1990, according to the United States Weather Bureau. Robert Schindler clearly remembers the sky turning light as they drove to the hospital.

Approximately 7:00 A.M.—Robert and Mary Schindler arrive at Humana Northside Hospital. Terri is being treated in the emergency room.

Approximately 7:30 A.M.—Mary calls her daughter Suzanne and tells her of Terri's condition. Suzanne begins the two-hour drive from Orlando to St. Petersburg.

MICHAEL SCHIAVO'S STATEMENTS

Michael Schiavo is the only witness to describe the circumstances surrounding Terri's collapse. The victim herself remained incapable of communicating up until her death fifteen years later. This means Michael's statements are the only eyewitness evidence directly relating to the incident. Michael has spoken to doctors on at least two occasions. He has given three depositions and testified in two trials. He also provided an extended description of the events of February 25, 1990, during his appearance on *Larry King Live*. (He has refused to speak with me, despite requests through his lawyer George Felos and his brother Scott.) Since Michael's are the only eyewitness reports, and they raise more questions than they answer, Michael's public statements regarding his observations and actions the night his wife collapsed deserve to be quoted in their entirety.

February 25, 1990, history and physical report by Dr. Samir Shah, Humana Hospital Northside:

"Her husband heard a bang about 6 A.M. and found his wife on the floor with difficulty breathing gasping for air and unresponsive. The paramedics were called right away which took them about three minutes. Resuscitation was started which took about 30 to 35 minutes and she was brought into the emergency room here where resuscitation was continued."

February 25, 1990, neurological consultation report by Dr. G. DeSousa, Humana Hospital Northside:

"This morning around 5 o'clock or so the husband heard a loud thump. When he went to check on his wife, he found her in the hallway unconscious and comatose. The paramedics were called in who rapidly arrived and they started to resuscitate the patient

who was found in a comatose state with cardiac arrhythmia, I believe."

**February 25, 1990, consultation report by Dr. David Kohl,
Humana Hospital Northside:**

"This unfortunate 26-year-old woman arrested in her home this
morning. Her husband found her unresponsive. The rescue squad
was summoned and found her at 5:52. Their resuscitative efforts
over the next 42 minutes included multiple doses of Epinephrine as
well as Lidocaine and Narcan. She required defibrillation on several occasions prior to arrival in the emergency room at 6:46 A.M."

**January 29, 1991, statement to Dr. James Carnahan,
Mediplex Rehab, Bradenton:**

"Mike states that Terry got up early on the morning of February
25, 1990 and went into their bathroom. He heard her fall, landing
'mostly' in the hall. He saw what he thought was vomitus (later
proved to be from one of the cats) so he rolled her to her side but
couldn't rouse her. She appeared to be gasping for breath, Mike
called 911."

July 27, 1992, deposition for medical malpractice trial:

A. I didn't get in until like 12:30, something like that, 1:00. We
had late parties that day at the restaurant.

Q. Was your wife awake when you got in?

A. No.

Q. Did you talk to her at all before you went to bed?

A. She said good night to me.

Q. Okay. In other words, you went—you crawled in bed and she said good night.

A. Yep.

Q. What's the next thing you recall after that?

A. Next thing I recall is I'm getting out of bed for some reason, and I heard her fall and hit the floor.

Q. You were getting out of bed?

A. For some reason.

Q. How far is the bed from the place where she fell?

A. About seven feet.

Q. What kind of floor are we talking about, carpeted or—

A. Carpeted, yes.

Q. Okay. And where was it that she fell?

A. In the hallway outside the bathroom door.

Q. Were her feet still in the bathroom?

A. I don't recall if they were or not; I don't think so.

Q. Could you tell whether or not from where she was positioned if she had—was coming from the bathroom?

A. I couldn't tell.

Q. Was the bathroom light on?

A. Yes.

Q. Is it normally kept on overnight?

A. No, it's not.

Q. Would it then be fair to assume that she had turned it on?

A. She would have to, yes.

Q. Okay. Was there any sound in the bathroom that you heard, either before or after you—after she fell that would indicate that she might have been using either the sink or the toilet in the bathroom?

A. No sounds at all.

Q. How was she dressed?

A. She had a night shirt on with pants, with—

Q. Underpants?

A. I think they were sweat pants.

Q. Oh, okay. Sweat pants?

A. Yeah.

Q. Was the night shirt something she would have slept in?

A. Yes. Yeah.

Q. How about the sweat pants?

A. She slept in them.

Q. She slept in sweat pants and a night shirt?

A. Oh, yeah.

Q. Okay. It's cold in February, oh, yeah.

A. It's cold.

Q. So that would have been her sleeping attire?

A. Some nights, yes.

Q. Okay. Were there any other lights on that you noticed beside [*sic*] the bathroom light?

A. Yes.

Q. What other light?

A. It was just a night light that we have out in the kitchen that goes on when it gets dark.

Q. Okay. That wasn't one that someone would have turned on?

A. No. No.

Q. Other than that, were there any other lights on?

A. No.

Q. Did you hear her when she got out of bed?

A. No, I did not.

Q. Do you know why she got out of bed?

A. Looks like she was doing something with the cats.

Q. You had some cats?

A. Uh-huh.

Q. That's a yes?

A. Yes.

Q. Okay. Were the cats in the house at the time?

A. Yes.

Q. How many cats did you have?

A. Two.

Q. You said something with the cats, what do you mean by that, playing with them or letting them out or what?

A. Could be. No. They were indoor cats.

Q. Okay. Why do you say it looks like she was doing something with the cats?

A. Because they both came walking out of the bathroom when I ran out there.

Q. Oh, okay.

A. They could have jumped over her or whatever. I don't know if she was doing something with the cats or not.

Q. Oh, okay.

A. It just looked to be like she was.

Q. Now, what—when you saw her, do you know what time it was?

A. I believe it was almost five a.m.

Q. When you saw her, how was she lying; in other words, on her back or—

A. On her back.

Q. Did she make any sound at all before she fell that you heard?

A. No, not—I didn't hear any sounds before she fell.

Q. What did you do then, after you—

A. After she fell?

Q. After you found her in the hallway?

A. I was—I was to her within two seconds. I seen she stopped breathing, I ran to the phone, called 911 within five seconds and panicked.

Q. What did you do then, after that?

A. I went over to her. I—I thought maybe—I just started talking to her and holding her; I didn't know what to do.

Q. Did you try any CPR?

A. No.

Q. You mentioned you saw that she stopped breathing. What did you do?

A. When she stopped breathing?

Q. No. No. No. How did you determine that, that she had stopped breathing?

A. Because I felt her chest and I heard her gasp once, you know, and—

Q. Okay. Then what happened?

A. I immediately went over and called 911.

Q. Okay. After—after 911 and after you were holding her, what was—what then happened, was the next thing that happened?

A. I laid Terry down, I went over and called my—I remember my brother-in-law lived in the same complex; I called him.

Q. Called brother-in-law?

A. Uh-huh.

Q. What is his name?

A. Robert.

Q. Schindler?

A. Correct.

Q. And what happened then, who came first?

A. He was there within minutes, within—I'm sorry, seconds, because he just lived right around the corner, and as soon as he came up, the paramedics pulled up.

Q. How long did it take the paramedics to get there.

A. Four minutes, five minutes; at the most, six, seven minutes.

Q. What did you and Robert do, if anything—

A. Nothing.

Q. —before the paramedics got there?

A. Nothing we could do. I didn't know what to do.

Q. Okay. And then what happened? It's my understanding that the fire department got there first and then the paramedics came; do you recall that?

A. I don't recall that at all.

Q. Okay.

A. I'm sorry, yeah, the fire department—the paramedic fire department—

Q. Right.

A. —got there first.

Q. Right. And what happened then?

A. They looked her over and started CPR and—

Q. Okay.

A. And I went out and I was just spastic in the living room.

November 15, 1992, testimony in medical malpractice trial:
Q. What time of day did you see her on the 24th?

A. Late at night.

Q. Okay. Would that be when you got off work?

A. It was a Saturday night, so probably 11:30, 12:00 by the time I got home.

Q. Where were you working at that time?

A. Agostino's restaurant.

Q. What time did they close the restaurant?

A. Stopped serving 10:00, and if people were walking in a quarter to ten, they serve them.

Q. You recall approximately what time you got home that evening?

A. 11:30, 12:00.

Q. Your wife up?

A. I don't recall if she was up or not.

Q. Do you recall whether or not you had any conversation with her that night?

A. I might have. I don't remember that conversation.

Q. Okay. Would it be fair to assume that you don't recall anything out of the ordinary happening as far as your wife, her condition or anything about her that evening?

A. Nothing out of the ordinary, no.

Q. She seemed fine to you; is that correct?

A. Yes.

Q. When was the last time you saw her before you went to bed that night, in other words, when you, after you got off from Agostino's?

A. The last time I saw her? Rephrase that question.

Q. That was a Saturday, was it, not the 24th?

A. Yes.

Q. So, she did not work; is that correct?

A. No, she didn't.

Q. What time did you get up to go to work?

A. Being it was a Saturday, Friday night I probably got home late, I usually don't get up until 10:00, 10:30.

Q. Okay. Do you recall whether or not she was there when you got up?

A. No, she usually did her food shopping when I was sleeping.

Q. You don't recall seeing her that morning?

A. Not that early.

Q. All right. Up to the time of her collapse, what was her condition as far as you can observe?

A. What do you mean by condition?

Q. Did she seem healthy, the same old Terri?

A. She seemed like my wife.

Q. Okay. Well, you know, did she seem healthy is actually my question?

A. To me, yeah.

January 24, 2000, testimony in guardianship trial:
Q. Michael, tell me what occurred on February 25, 1990.

A. I got home late from work that night. I came in the house. Terri woke up. She heard me. I gave her a kiss good night. She gave me a kiss good night. A few hours later, I was getting out of bed for some reason and I heard this thud. So I ran out into the hall and I found Terri on the floor. I knelt down next to her and I turned her over because she sort of fell on her face. On her stomach and face. I turned her over going, "Terri, Terri. You okay?" She kind of had this gurgling noise. I laid her down and ran over and called 911. I was hysterical. I called 911. I called her brother, who lived in the same complex as we did. I ran back to Terri. She was not moving. I held her in my arms until her brother got there. I rocked her. I didn't know what to do. I was hysterical. It was a horrible moment.

Q. Do you know how long it was before the paramedics came?

A. Had to be a good six minutes or so.

Q. What happened when the paramedics came?

A. I moved away. Her brother was sitting in the kitchen around the corner. I moved away and they started working on Terri. They put the leads on. I heard them say she is flat line. Start CPR. I am standing there going what is happening here? Why is this happening? Why isn't her heart beating? I was just a mess. I was hysterical.

Larry King Live, October 27, 2003:

> KING: Let's go back. What happened, Michael, on February 25, 1990?
>
> SCHIAVO: I work late at night. I used to run—manage restaurants. I came home around 2:00 in the morning, climbed into bed.
>
> KING: No children?
>
> SCHIAVO: No children. Terri and I were trying to have children. We were back and forth to a doctor for a year or so, trying to find out why we weren't getting pregnant.
>
> . . . climbed into bed. Terri said good night to me. Gave me a kiss. She woke up, said good night, gave me a kiss. I gave her a kiss back. I'd say, about 4:30 in the morning, I was, for some reason, getting out of bed and I heard a thud in the hall. I race out there and Terri was laying in the hall. I went down to get her. I thought, well, maybe she just tripped or whatever. I rolled her over

and she was lifeless. And it almost seems like she had this last breath.

So I held her in my arms, and I'm trying to shake her up. I ran over, I called 911. Her brother happened to live in the same complex as we did. I called him. I went back to Terri. And from there, six, seven minutes later, the paramedics . . .

KING: And the way she is now is the way she was that night?

SCHIAVO: That night she was totally unconscious.

KING: And later what developed? She opened her eyes open?

SCHIAVO: Probably about a month later, she opened her eyes.

Considered together, these are confusing and self-contradictory statements that require explanation. Unfortunately, the closer we look at them, the more suspicion they cast on Michael Schiavo.

CHAPTER ELEVEN

Michael's Story

When Michael Schiavo first picked up the phone to summon help for his unconscious wife, he began a chain of evidence that in the initial drama of saving Terri's life was overlooked by family, the paramedics, and police.

The statements of a witness are important evidence, especially if that witness becomes a suspect down the road. In a case that lacks meaningful forensic evidence, the statements of the only witness are the most powerful clues that something suspicious or possibly criminal has occurred.

Witnesses often don't tell the whole truth. Sometimes their failure to do so is perfectly innocent. They're trying to hide an embarrassing fact, or they forget something in the stress of the moment. Sometimes it's not so innocent—they're trying to hide their complicity in some other criminal activity. Sometimes it's deliberate deception because they are responsible for the crime being investigated.

When do statements that are based on partial truths or even total lies become deceptions? How can they shown to be intentional or manipulative?

When there is no malice or criminality, these questions tend to answer themselves over time. If the explanation is innocent, or at least not criminal, the facts usually surface through police investigation, interrogations, or even unprovoked confessions. A witness admits that the reason he can't account for his time was that he had been visiting a girlfriend, or somebody accounts for forensic transfer evidence like hair or fiber by stating that they did, contrary to previous statements, touch the victim prior to notifying the police.

In the Terri Schiavo case, the inconsistencies in the statements of the only witness able to give his version of events were never challenged. Not by the paramedics or the police or the doctors or other family members or any of the lawyers in the long legal history that followed. Following the 2000 guardian trial, one of the Schindlers' lawyers, Pat Anderson, tried to depose him four times and each time he failed to appear.

The only line of questioning focusing on Michael Schiavo's possible criminal involvement occurred when a police officer asked Robert Schindler if he thought Michael had anything to do with Terri's collapse. Bob said, "No. No way." The police heard the results of the blood screen and CAT scan, determined that Terri hadn't been on drugs or suffered a violent blow to the head. They probably hung out at the nurses' lounge, drinking coffee until the end of their watch, and then went home. The case was passed on to homicide, but since Terri didn't die, there was no follow-up.

Michael's statements, beginning with his first description of the events that morning in the hospital, when his memory should have been fresh, are filled with inconsistencies and are contradicted by other evidence or witness statements. He related events about the collapse of his wife several different times that morning. He spoke to the paramedics, the police, and at least one doctor, Dr. Samir Shah, at Humana Northside Hospital (he might have spoken to others, although he doesn't recall doing so). At the apartment, he spoke with Bobby Schindler. In the hospital waiting room, he spoke to Robert, Mary, Suzanne, and Bobby Schindler as well as two friends of Terri's, Jackie Rhodes and Mary Anne Nicholson. Almost a year later he spoke to Dr. James Carnahan at Mediplex Rehab. Subsequently, he gave three depositions and testified in two separate trials, as well as appearing on *Larry King Live*.

Michael Schiavo has no problem telling people what happened, he just can't seem to remember what he last said.

When did he find Terri?

The most important question is the most easily answered. What time did you find your wife unconscious? This is probably the most important fact of those early hours of February 25, 1990. I don't think it's unreasonable to expect Michael to remember, or at least be consistent.

Michael's report of discovering Terri at 4:30 to 5:00 A.M. is a human estimate contradicted by the hard evidence of the 911 call and the hospital and police records. It can also be contradicted by a logical re-creation of the time line counting back from the arrival of Robert and Mary Schindler at Humana Hospital.

They arrived at the hospital as the sun was rising, approximately 7:00 A.M. It was a twenty-minute drive, so they left around 6:40. According to their recollections, it took them ten minutes to get ready (they hadn't gotten dressed as they waited for Bobby to call back). That puts Bobby's phone call at around 6:30. The 911 call came in at 5:40 and the paramedics arrived at 5:52. So Michael had to have called the Schindlers before 5:40 if Robert is remembering correctly and if Michael told Jackie Rhodes the truth when he said he called the Schindlers before calling 911.

No matter how you look at it, Michael is missing at least forty minutes. The gap from either 4:30 or 5:00 A.M. until the 911 call at 5:40 A.M. is a very long time, particularly when the victim is suffering cardiorespiratory arrest. This is important not only for a criminal investigation, but also for Terri's medical treatment and any decisions made by paramedics and doctors. Time is of the essence, and a couple minutes, even seconds, could be the difference between life and death. If Terri's brain had been deprived of oxygen for more than five minutes, she would have suffered severe and irreversible brain damage. If she had suffered oxygen deprivation for as much as ten minutes, she would be dead—or close to it.

It is possible that Terri's oxygen deprivation was gradual or partial, and she lay on the floor unconscious for a very long time. Her heart could have been beating feebly, with her brain receiving only a fraction of the oxygen it needed, resulting in damage that occurred more slowly over a longer period.

The paramedics probably didn't ask Michael when he found her, assuming it was just prior to the 911 call. The Humana Hospital reports quote 5:00 and 6:00 A.M. as the times when Michael discovered her. Dr. Shah stated that Michael found Terri at 6:00 A.M., but this might not be based on a direct statement by Michael. Instead, it looks like Shah was counting backwards from a 6:46 arrival time at the hospital after forty-two minutes of resuscitation by the paramedics. (This time estimate doesn't include the twelve-minute drive from the apartment to the hospital or the response time after the 911 call, further indication that it is guesswork on the part of the doctor.) Dr. DeSousa's report quotes 5:00 A.M. Dr. Kohl's report does not state a time when Michael discovered Terri, but is obviously counting backward from the paramedic run sheet and emergency-room arrival time.

Michael's missing forty minutes must be explained. Was he mistaken about the time? Then why didn't he revise his statements? If he is correct, then what was he doing between the time he saw Terri lying on the floor unconscious and his phone calls to Robert Schindler and the 911 operator?

Was Michael intentionally lying when he said he found his wife sometime between 4:30 and 5:00 A.M.? I don't think so.

Dr. Shah's report noted that the paramedics were summoned

and arrived at 5:52 A.M. Michael had access to this document (it was initially part of the malpractice trial and kept by his lawyers for subsequent legal procedures), but apparently never noticed how it contradicted his own statements about that morning. He also had access to the paramedic run sheet, which was never turned over to the Schindlers and lists the arrival time.

The police report written by Officer Brewer was never requested by anyone until 2003, when Suzanne Vitadamo hired private investigator Kurt Klein to look into her sister's case. Klein had some contacts at the St. Petersburg police. He made a few phone calls. At first he was told that the report was no longer part of the system and there was no record it had even been written. Then Klein wound up talking with Officer Brewer himself, who was working as a desk sergeant. Brewer was able to find his original report on microfiche, but it was very degenerated. Klein was able to read it, but could not make a copy. So he retyped the report verbatim, saying that "this new entry is absolutely accurate as to the content of the narrative."

Brewer's report lists the call occurrence as 5:40 A.M., the time the police were dispatched as 6:11 A.M., and the time police arrived as 6:33 A.M.

This report was never seen by anyone but the St. Petersburg police prior to October 22, 2003. Ironically, it soon became available on the Terri Schiavo Web site. Michael never again cooperated and allowed himself to be deposed even though he was subpoenaed several times. (I'm assuming he had not read the police report prior to his appearance on *Larry King Live* only five days after the report was discovered.) Michael has had fifteen years to think about it, and yet he never changed his statement that he found Terri at or before 5:00 A.M.

Why did he never adjust his time estimate closer to the documented 911 call? Because nobody ever questioned him about it.

If Michael is telling the truth and remembering correctly, what happened between his discovery of Terri at 4:30 to 5:00 A.M. and his 5:40 call to 911? In several statements he described himself as panicking. Could his panic have lasted for forty-five minutes, or even longer?

> *"He told us that he heard her fall, and he lay in bed and said, Terri, Terri. When she didn't respond to him, he got up and found her on the bathroom floor."*
>
> —JACKIE RHODES

Here is another version, Jackie Rhodes and Mary Ann Nicholson say Michael told them in the ICU waiting room at Humana Hospital. This adds another twist, which is negligence, whether intentional or accidental. If this statement is true, how long did he lie there? Why does he say in later statements that he ran to her "in seconds"?

Why did he wake up?

Michael has repeatedly stated that he got out of bed "for some reason" when he heard a thud. He has also said that he woke up because he heard the thud.

Who gets out of bed "for some reason"? Did Michael have to go to the bathroom? If so, why doesn't he say that? Is he afraid to say he was going to the bathroom because he doesn't want to place himself there?

Why isn't he clear as to what woke him up? Why would he wake up and get out of bed prior to hearing the thud? Why doesn't he seem to remember which came first, his waking up or hearing the thud?

Jackie Rhodes said that Michael told her at Humana Hospital that Terri had woken up to clean the cats' rear ends. He said that he had observed "black stuff and toilet paper" in the toilet, which is what made him arrive at that conclusion. Also at the hospital, Michael told Mary Schindler that he thought Terri had gotten up to feed the cats. In the medical malpractice deposition, Michael also mentions the cats, but here he is even more vague.

Q. Did you hear her when she got out of bed?

A. No, I did not.

Q. Do you know why she got out of bed?

A. Looks like she was doing something with the cats.

Later in that deposition:

Q. Okay. Why do you say it looks like she was doing something with the cats?

A. Because they both came walking out of the bathroom when I ran out there.

Q. Oh, okay.

A. They could have jumped over her or whatever. I don't know if she was doing something with the cats or not.

No mention of his being in the bathroom and observing "black stuff and toilet paper" in the toilet. His statements about viewing the toilet put Michael in the bathroom around the time of Terri's collapse. What was he doing there? Why does he not mention this in other statements?

Since Terri gave the cats dry food and kept their bowls full, it's highly unlikely that she would wake up at 5 A.M. to feed them. More probably, she would have filled the bowls before going to bed. While everybody describes her as being devoted to her pets, isn't waking up at five in the morning to wipe them just a little obsessive?

Dr. James Carnahan at Mediplex Rehabilitation in Bradenton wrote this after an interview with Michael when Terri was being admitted to that facility on January 29, 1991.

> "Mike states that Terry [sic] got up early on the morning of February 25, 1990 and went into their bathroom. He heard her fall, landing 'mostly' in the hall. He saw what he thought was vomitus (later proved to be from one of the cats) so he rolled her to her side but couldn't rouse her. She appeared to be gasping for breath, Mike called 911."
>
> —DR. JAMES CARNAHAN

This statement raises another series of questions: Why didn't Michael mention vomit in any of his other statements? Who determined that it was cat vomit? Why doesn't it show up in any of the Humana Hospital reports? Why don't any of the other witnesses remember him saying this? Why, in all of the controversy surrounding her alleged bulimia, was this never introduced as evidence?

Why did he think Terri had fallen?

Michael Schiavo is consistent with one aspect of his story. He says he heard a thud and thought Terri had fallen. Sometimes he says that he woke up prior to hearing the thud and sometimes he says the thud woke him up. But he always states that when he heard the thud, he thought Terri had fallen. His wife was a healthy twenty-six-year-old woman with no preexisting medical condition. Why would Michael think she had fallen at the mere sound of a thud, especially if it woke him from his sleep?

Terri's two cats lived inside the house. Their litter box was in the bathroom. I have two cats who sleep all day and chase each other at night. If I am ever woken up in the middle of the night, my first thought is that it's the cats. My second thought would be a burglar.

One possibility is that Terri had been ill recently and Michael was afraid that something might have happened to her. Michael later said told police "she had been tired lately and not feeling well." Terri's parents had seen her the night before, and aside from the yeast infection, she seemed to be in good health. Even if his wife was tired and not feeling well, why would that make Michael think she had collapsed when he heard a bump in the night?

What position was Terri in when he found her?

In his deposition for the medical malpractice trial, Michael described Terri lying "on her back." During the January 22, 2000, guardianship trial, he testified: "I turned her over because she sort of fell on her face. On her stomach and face." On *Larry King Live*, Michael said, "I rolled her over . . ." which indicates she was face-down when he found her.

When Bobby Schindler entered the apartment he saw his sister lying facedown.

When the paramedics arrived, Bobby moved out of their way and joined Michael in the living room.

"They found a subject in question [Theresa] lying face down . . ."
— POLICE REPORT

Michael is not able to remember if his wife was faceup or facedown when he found her, even with the help of legal counsel preparing him for court appearances.

If you discovered a loved one unconscious on the floor in the early morning, don't you think you'd remember if she was faceup or facedown? Wouldn't the image of how you first saw her be etched in your memory, and be vivid and consistent every time you described it?

Did he pick her up?

In his medical malpractice deposition, Michael said the following:

Q. After you found her in the hallway?

A. I was—I was to her within two seconds. I seen she stopped breathing, I ran to the phone, called 911 within five seconds and panicked.

Q. What did you do then, after that?

A. I went over to her. I—I thought maybe—I just started talking to her and holding her; I didn't know what to do.

In the guardianship trial:

> I knelt down next to her and I turned her over because she sort of fell on her face. On her stomach and face. I turned her over going, "Terri, Terri. You okay?" She kind of had this gurgling noise. I laid her down and ran over and called 911. I was hysterical. I called 911. I called her brother, who lived in the same complex as we did. I ran back to Terri. She was not moving. I held her in my arms until her brother got there. I rocked her. I didn't know what to do. I was hysterical. It was a horrible moment.

On *Larry King Live*, Michael said: "So I held her in my arms, and I'm trying to shake her up."

Michael's descriptions of how he picked Terri up and held her are not consistent with Bobby's clear recollection that after Michael answered the door, he, Bobby, went over to Terri and remained with her until the paramedics arrived while Michael paced the hallway.

If Michael picked Terri off the floor and held her until Bobby came, why did Bobby see her facedown? Did Michael place her back on the floor facedown? He would have had to in order for both Bobby and the paramedics to see Terri in that position.

In the guardianship trial, Michael stated that once Bobby arrived, he picked Terri up again and held her until the paramedics showed up. He said that Bobby remained in the kitchen.

Q. What happened when the paramedics came?

A. I moved away. Her brother was sitting in the kitchen around the corner. I moved away and they started working on Terri.

Does this mean that he picked Terri up once, laid her back down on her face to answer the door when Bobby arrived, and then picked her up again, only to lay her back down on her face when the paramedics came? How did the paramedics enter the apartment (Bobby says he didn't get the door because he stayed with Terri)? Who was nearest Terri's body when they arrived?

Did Michael pick her up or not? If he did, why did he put her back facedown? If he didn't, why did he make statements to that effect? Was he trying to account for missing time between his discovery of Terri and the 911 call? Was he trying to account for any possible bruises on her body? Or was he trying to show himself as a proactive and compassionate husband caring for his stricken wife? If this last is the case, he should have given her CPR.

Why didn't he perform CPR?

The day after Terri was first admitted, Jackie Rhodes came to Humana Hospital. In the ICU waiting room with Mary Ann Nicholson, she asked Michael if he knew CPR. He said that he did. She asked him why he hadn't administered it. Michael said that he panicked. Jackie has testified to this and confirmed it to me herself. Mary Ann Nicholson corroborated Jackie's recollection when I spoke with her.

In 1992, Cindy Brashers Shook asked Michael why he hadn't performed CPR on Terri. He said that he had panicked. As a restaurant manager, and alumnus of McDonald's Hamburger University, Michael should have known CPR. While Cindy has denied several statements she reportedly made about Michael, she confirmed this conversation.

Either Michael knew CPR or he didn't. If he didn't know it, why wouldn't he admit that to Jackie Rhodes and Marianne Nicholson? I believe it's more likely that he did know CPR and was embarrassed to admit to Cindy Brashers Shook that he had panicked. McDonald's manager training includes CPR. Restaurants in the United States are required by law to have posters describing CPR in an employee area.

Even if he didn't know CPR, in a case where the victim is unconscious and not breathing, the 911 operator will usually ask the caller if he knows CPR and talk him through it if he doesn't.

Whom did he call first?

Why does Michael insist that he phoned Bobby Schindler shortly after calling 911? Michael repeatedly stated that he first called 911, then Bobby Schindler, because he lived nearby. In his official statements, Michael has never admitted to calling Robert Schindler first, and he never says that Robert Schindler told him to call 911. When he saw Mary Ann Nicholson at the hospital, he told her he had called Terri's parents first.

Robert and Mary Schindler both remember it very clearly. The phone rang in the early morning. Robert answered. Michael was on the line. Sounding very nervous and upset, he told Robert that something had happened to Terri. Robert told him to hang up and call 911. Then Robert called Bobby and told him to go over to the Schiavos' apartment because something had happened to Terri. Some twenty minutes later, according to their recollection (it was probably longer), Bobby called them back to say Terri was being taken to the hospital.

After hearing Michael say that he had called Bobby first, Bobby testified in the 2000 guardianship trial that Michael called him. When he spoke with his parents afterward, Bobby realized he had been mistaken. I think the timeline proves that Robert Schindler was correct in his recollection.

If Michael had called 911 just prior to calling Bobby, then Bobby would have arrived well before the paramedics. Bobby says, "I got my clothes on and hauled ass over there." If the first call went out at 5:40, then Bobby would have arrived at the apartment around 5:42, maybe as late as 5:44, some eight to ten minutes before the paramedics, who had a twelve-minute drive to the apartment. Bobby describes the paramedics arriving only a minute or two after he did.

Bobby called his parents just prior to Terri's being transported to the hospital at 6:34. He remembers making the phone call from the living room of Terri's apartment. She still wasn't stabilized and the paramedics continued CPR even as they were taking her down out to the ambulance. Stopping to administer CPR and possibly other emergency treatments, the paramedics might have needed several minutes to get her into the ambulance and take off for the hospital. Because they were not expecting to go to the hospital, Robert and Mary were not ready to leave immediately. They left their house some eight to ten minutes after receiving Bobby's phone call, as they still had to get dressed. The sun was beginning to rise as they made the twenty-minute drive to the hospital. When they got there, it was light. Official sunrise that day was 6:59 A.M.

What reason could Michael have for not admitting that he first called Robert Schindler?

Michael might have gotten Robert and Bobby mixed up. But Michael has testified several times that he called Bobby because he lived nearby, which indicates he did not confuse them.

Michael simply forgot. I don't find this credible, considering the fact that over the next fifteen years numerous legal procedures have required his sworn statements following preparation with his lawyers.

Michael was embarrassed to have panicked while Terri's life was in danger. This is human error with no malice or criminal intent. Presented with a stressful situation, people sometimes lose control of themselves and make mistakes. Michael has repeatedly said that he panicked. Robert Schindler described his voice as being nervous and worried. Bobby said Michael was "freaking out." Bobby wasn't as worried, because he saw Terri was breathing. (Michael has testified both to her breathing and not breathing, but if Bobby saw her breathing, then we can assume that she was.)

Michael didn't call Bobby because he didn't want someone to come immediately. Robert Schindler was on the other side of town—Bobby was across the courtyard. We often see suspects avoid or delay the moment of contact with police, ambulance, or family members until the last possible moment. In this way, they resemble little kids, thinking that if they can delay getting in trouble, it will somehow be easier.

This last possibility is entirely speculative, but must be considered. It does not mean that Michael Schiavo had criminal involvement, only that his behavior might resemble that of a person with a guilty conscience.

Suspects know when they have problems with time. The first call to Robert would have stopped the clock and established Michael's state of mind, which was panic. The call to Robert would also buy time as Terri's parents were at least fifteen to twenty minutes away if they left immediately. Perhaps Michael did not want anyone in the apartment until paramedics arrived. When Bobby appeared it must have been a surprise to Michael, since he would not have known that Bobby had been called.

DOMESTIC DISPUTES

The police asked Michael if he and Terri had had any arguments lately and he told them "no major ones." That question had to be asked at the hospital, since the police arrived at the apartment just before Terri was being transported, and they went to the hospital to follow up. No police officer asked Michael any more questions after that morning.

Are we supposed to believe that this young husband—who was so hysterical and panic stricken that he couldn't administer CPR, or even think to call 911, and is now waiting to see if his wife will survive—would be capable of playing with words during a police interview?

I have interviewed many people who are experiencing these circumstances. It is a delicate and uncomfortable situation to interview the husband or any close family member of someone who has recently had an accident that might be suspicious, or might not.

As a cop, you have to figure out whether there might possibly have been any criminal action. And you have to do it by asking questions of the very people who are secondary victims—the family and close friends.

If I had been the investigating officer and Michael Schiavo told me he and his wife hadn't had any major arguments, I would have asked him: "What do you mean by major fights?" Often a suspect will admit something little and apparently harmless before confessing to the crime itself. Was Michael trying to get something off his chest? Did the fact that he and Terri fought the day before bother him—whether or not it resulted in the direct cause of her collapse? Was he feeling guilty because the last words he spoke to his wife had been in anger? Was he simply embarrassed that their marriage—like every other relationship—wasn't perfect?

"No major ones" is a hint that there had been a fight. If there wasn't a fight, he would have said no. If the fight was not a source of guilt for him, he could have told the officer about it.

Michael knew he'd had an argument with Terri the day before she collapsed. Michael knew what the argument was about and how serious it was (whether or not he'd choose to characterize it as "major"). What he didn't know was whether Terri had told anybody about it.

> "The malpractice attorney followed me down to the pay phone
> and said to me, You know, it wouldn't help the case at all if I told
> them that Theresa and Michael were talking about getting a
> divorce. I turned to him and I said if I'm asked that question and
> that is the correct answer, that is the answer I'm going to give."
> —JACKIE RHODES, TESTIMONY, JANUARY 26, 2000

Rhodes was not asked any questions on the subject, and so there was no testimony concerning her knowledge of the February 24 argument until the guardianship trial in 2000.

In all of Michael's statements concerning the day before Terri's collapse, he never mentions the fight. One time he seems to imply that he didn't see her that Saturday, and in descriptions of when he came home, he says they kissed and said they loved each other. This might well be true, but why did Michael never mention the argument with Terri?

Was the argument resolved when Michael went to work that night? When Terri saw Bobby in the afternoon, she told him she and Michael had been fighting. When she returned to Bobby's apartment after mass and dinner with her parents, Terri said couldn't go out that night because she wanted to be home when Michael got back. "Michael held on to stuff," Bobby says. He has been described by several Schindler family members as hypersensitive and willing to hold a grudge for a long time.

Was Terri waiting up for Michael when he returned? Did Michael call her from work, as he was known to have done in the past? Did the argument pick up again when Michael came home? When did Michael come home? Did they go to bed, or stay up arguing until the early morning hours? Could the stress of a major domestic dispute have been a contributing factor in Terri's collapse?

WHEN WITNESSES MAKE MISTAKES

Michael has repeatedly claimed that he does not have a very good memory. The accurate remembrance of time is understandably confusing for Michael since he was under extreme stress, even shock, at discovering Terri collapsed and unconscious on the floor. Yet even in the most stressful situations, the events just prior to the discovery of an unconscious loved one should be accurate and easily corroborated. The problems with Michael's statements are not limited to his recollections after he discovered Terri, but also before. He has said they didn't have a fight. He is vague about whether or not he saw her that afternoon.

In twenty years of law enforcement, I learned that perceptions can be altered under stress, producing some ridiculous claims. Yet such claims almost always pertain to unknowns, not knowns. You see it all the time in robbery cases, where the victim is frightened, even traumatized. When you interview the victim, even right after the robbery, he can't give you a description of the suspect or remember whether or not he had a gun.

This is not the same thing. There is no threat of physical harm. Obviously, there is stress, but the type of emotional fear that victims experience is not present in Michael Schiavo's case. My experience is that the recollections of family members who discover loved ones dead or injured are usually very accurate. They remember vivid details that remain with them for the rest of their lives. This is the case in Bobby Schindler's recollection. Why isn't Michael's the same? He spent even more time with Terri. He was the first one to see her. Instead of being vivid and accurate, his recollections are vague, contradictory, and sometimes nonsensical. The story changes every time he tells it.

What is Michael Schiavo afraid of?

Looking at the problems with Michael Schiavo's recollections of the events leading up to and including the collapse of his wife, I am led to one conclusion. He is intentionally misstating certain facts because he has something to hide. It might be something perfectly innocent, such as feeling guilty that the last conversation he had with his wife was a fight over her hair color. It might be something more suspicious, such as wanting to cover up possible criminal involvement or negligence in her collapse.

Michael's only consistent recollection from the early morning hours of February 25, 1990, is the sound of Terri falling to the floor, which he consistently describes as a thud.

Why does he remember this detail, while everything else is vague or contradictory?

Whether or not he committed a criminal act, I believe Michael witnessed Terri falling. And he has never forgotten that.

CHAPTER TWELVE

Possible Scenarios

The collapse of Terri Schiavo has only so many scenarios, which can be narrowed down even further to two basic possibilities: Either she collapsed because of some accident or organic bodily insult, or she was assaulted.

There was no meaningful forensic transfer evidence in this case because the only possible suspect is Terri's husband. Considering that Michael lived at the location of her collapse, his forensic contributions of hair, saliva, sperm, and fingerprints are useless. Even if another suspect did mysteriously surface, no forensic evidence was ever collected.

There was no medical forensic evidence in this case because Terri Schiavo didn't die until March 31, 2005. Had she died in close proximity to the time of her collapse, there would have been an autopsy, which might have provided evidence indicating why she collapsed. Even if the autopsy had taken place the day after her collapse, doctors might not have been able to distinguish, for example, between sudden cardiac death due to arrhythmia or carotid choke-hold strangulation.

Now, fifteen years after the event, we have even less physical evidence. The autopsy will be conducted and hopefully the medical examiner will find something conclusive, although that possibility is remote.

Instead, we are reduced to piecing together witness statements, medical records, science, and perhaps a little common sense to try to solve the mystery that lies locked within Terri Schiavo's heart and Michael Schiavo's memory.

When a detective team is working a case, they will often sit down, over coffee in the morning or beer at night, and think outside of the box, tossing around ideas that sometimes sound ridiculous, sometimes are ridiculous, and sometimes wind up solving the case.

The following scenarios are a look into my thought process—no different than if you, the reader, were my partner. Thinking out loud to refute as well as confirm certain conclusions. If you are someone who talks to yourself while engaged in an important task, you will understand. This is just a detective talking out loud, in the hope that by hearing his own words, the facts that he already knows backward and forward, will fit into some pattern that resembles the truth as it occurred.

SCENARIO #1

Terri Schiavo goes to bed sometime after 9:00 P.M. Saturday night and is not disturbed until her husband, Michael, comes home from work between 11:30 P.M. and 2:00 A.M. She awakes briefly to say good night and kiss him. At approximately 4:30 to 5:00 A.M., Terri gets up without disturbing Michael and goes to the bathroom. She turns on the bathroom light. Since it is a Sunday and she does not have to go to work, we can assume that she is not waking up for the day. She might have gotten up to urinate or because her yeast infection was bothering her.

Terri and Michael live in a small one-bedroom apartment. At 5:00 A.M., sunrise is two hours away. Terri does whatever it is she does in the bathroom and walks out, leaving the light on. The distance from where Terri collapsed to the bedroom is seven feet. The bedroom door is open, which means that the light in the bathroom illuminates the hall and even the bedroom somewhat.

Would Terri have left the bathroom light on knowing that her husband, who works nights, was still asleep? Small details like this are important. When you retrace Terri's movements, she had to be walking out of the bathroom when she collapsed into the hall with her feet and a portion of her legs still in the bathroom. Then it would appear that she collapsed exiting the bathroom, but before she could turn off the light switch.

When Bobby Schindler arrived at the apartment, he saw Terri facedown in the hall with her feet and part of her legs in the bathroom. Asked to sketch a diagram of the scene, Bobby drew his sister pointed toward the living room when she collapsed, not toward the bedroom.

Terri could have become light-headed as she exited the bathroom, fainted, and hit the floor. Her fall could have created the thud Michael has repeatedly described. Even a small noise is much louder in a quiet apartment.

Michael is awoken by the noise and gets up. Seeing the bathroom light on, he walks into the hall and sees Terri facedown on the floor. He kneels down and tries to revive her by turning her over and calling her name. Michael hears a gasping, gurgling breath and lays her down. He calls Robert Schindler, telling him Terri has collapsed and he can't wake her. Robert tells him to hang up and call 911. Michael thinks it is about 5:00 A.M.

Michael returns to Terri, but instead of giving her CPR, he just freezes. Minutes pass. Bobby Schindler arrives. He sees Terri gasping for breath. When the paramedics arrive a couple minutes later, Terri is no longer breathing and has no pulse.

Paramedics attempt to resuscitate Terri for forty-two minutes and are at least successful enough to transport her to Humana

Northside Hospital, where they arrive at 6:46 A.M. At the hospital, emergency-room personnel save Terri's life, but she remains unresponsive. Initials tests show no evidence of a heart attack, but do show a significant deficiency of potassium, a condition that could result in cardiac arrest.

Although there is little evidence to support the theory that Terri was bulimic, we also cannot eliminate it. Terri could have had a cardiac arrest brought on by the potassium imbalance and been deprived of oxygen to her brain long enough to cause irreparable brain damage.

SCENARIO #2

The initial conditions remain the same as the previous scenario up until the arrival of the paramedics. Terri has been unconscious for several minutes; she is struggling for breath. The paramedics initially connect her to an EKG, start an IV, establish a clear airway, and perform CPR. Their attempts at resuscitation include seven defibrillations in combination with manual CPR between each one, but Terri is nonresponsive. Then efforts continue for forty-two minutes before they transport Terri to the hospital.

Was Terri's brain deprived of oxygen during the emergency resuscitation procedures? Was her brain damage caused by the paramedics' inability to create a clear airway? Were they sure that air was getting to Terri's lungs? How long did Terri's heart beat between defibrillations? Did it beat at all between defib and CPR? Did the paramedics transport Terri without establishing a heart rhythm?

Seven years after the incident, SunStar Medic One destroyed all the records, with no backup archive. The run sheet that the paramedics used to document their treatment and the vital signs of the patient was not part of the collection of medical records turned over to the Schindler family lawyers.

Aside from a few questions put to fireman-paramedic Radeski, the paramedics were never interviewed by the police, nor were they deposed or used as witnesses in any court proceeding regarding Terri's initial medical treatment. In fact, both SunStar paramedics left that company within one year of the incident. They both moved out of state and left the health care field. Neither paramedic will talk about this case.

It is entirely possible that all of Terri's brain damage occurred during the emergency resuscitation efforts and transport to the hospital.

SCENARIO #3

As with the first two scenarios, the initial circumstances are the same up to the point when Michael hears the thud. Michael wakes up enough to realize he has heard something, but pauses to listen for another noise. When he hears nothing further, he falls back asleep. He does not notice or look to see if his wife is lying next to him, or he simply assumes that she has gone to the bathroom. He wakes up again a short time later at 5:30 to 5:35 A.M. and realizes that Terri is not in bed. Michael now realizes that the thud could somehow have been connected to Terri. He calls out her name several times, with no response. He gets up in a panic to find Terri on the floor. He flashes back to the sound and tries to remember how long ago he heard it. All he hears from Terri is a gurgling sound as she struggles to breathe.

Michael panics. He doesn't know what to do, so he calls Robert Schindler and tells him Terri has collapsed. Robert tells Michael to hang up and call 911. Michael hangs up and calls 911. It is about 5:40 A.M.

After getting the call from his father, Bobby arrives at the apartment and sees his sister lying facedown in the hall. Then the paramedics show up and start trying to resuscitate her. Michael sits on the couch, looking worried and wringing his hands. He feels guilty about not getting up when he heard the thud. When he hears one of the paramedics say, "I'd be surprised if she makes it to the hospital," he realizes he should have done something to try to save her life.

When questioned by the paramedics, police, and doctors, Michael maintains that he heard the thud and immediately ran to the sound and found his wife in the hallway. In every subsequent statement he is careful to say that he got out of bed as soon as he heard the noise, ran over to his wife, and called 911 immediately. The reason he has so much trouble keeping his story straight is that it's based on a falsehood necessitated by guilt.

SCENARIO #4

In this scenario, we begin a couple days earlier. If the interactions between Michael and Terri on Saturday are somewhat sketchy from Michael's recollections, they are more clear in the memories of Bobby Schindler and Jackie Rhodes.

On Friday, Terri was at work at the Prudential Insurance office. Her colleague and friend Jackie Rhodes had an adjacent desk, and the two talked often about their personal lives. Terri confided in Jackie several times about the problems with her marriage and expressed her desire to leave Michael. Jackie knew that Terri's husband wanted her to dye her hair back to her natural brown. Terri wanted to remain a blonde. They had fought about it. Terri had an appointment with the hairdresser for Saturday morning. It became a joke between the two girls when they left for the weekend: Was she going to come back to work on Monday as a blonde or a brunette?

Sometime between 2:00 and 3:00 P.M. on Saturday, Jackie calls Terri to find out what she had done. Terri had dyed her hair blond, but Michael got angry and they had fought about her hair and the fact that it cost eighty dollars. Terri is crying. Jackie offers to come over and visit, but Terri declines, saying she is going to see Bobby.

Terri goes to Bobby's and tells him that she and Michael had a fight, but doesn't go into details. Bobby can tell that Terri is very upset and asks her if she wants to go out with him and his roommate that evening. Terri declines the offer and says that she is going to mass and then dinner with their parents.

Terri is back home around 8:30 P.M. She waits for Michael to come home.

Michael returns sometime between 10:30 and 2:00 A.M.

Terri is in bed, but wakes up when Michael comes in. The fight they had had earlier that day is resumed. Terri storms out of the bedroom, closing the door behind her, so that Michael cannot see into the hallway from the bedroom. She goes into the bathroom. She is severely stressed and suffering from low potassium—whatever the cause. Her heart begins to flutter; she feels dizzy and weak. She opens the bathroom door and collapses.

In the bedroom, Michael hears a thud. He thinks that Terri has punched the wall or maybe thrown something. Whether through anger, stubbornness, or just no longer giving a damn, he doesn't get up to see what happened.

After several minutes, even as long as a half hour, Michael still hears nothing. He calls Terri's name. There is no response. Finally, he opens the bedroom door and sees her unconscious on the floor.

SCENARIO #5

There is no doubt that up to this point Michael's possible conduct could be construed as disappointing, or even passively abusive, but not criminal. Even the next possible scenario lacks criminality on face value.

The same details as the previous scenario apply here, except when Terri tries to go into the bathroom, Michael pursues her.

They struggle and fall into the hallway with Michael on top of Terri, his two hundred forty pounds landing on her back. She gets the wind knocked out of her, and the impact causes her heart, weakened already by low potassium, to begin fibrillating.

Michael immediately gets up and tries to revive Terri, but she does not respond. He becomes scared, apologizes, and calls out her name, but she lies there motionless. Michael doesn't know what to do. He sets her back facedown and goes into the living room, where he paces back and forth. Minutes pass. He is afraid to make the phone call, knowing this is his fault. With every minute he waits, it only gets worse. Forty minutes later he regains enough composure to call Robert Schindler at home.

SCENARIO #6

The same as the previous two scenarios, except that once they are inside the bathroom, the interaction between Terri and Michael becomes physical. Whether accidentally or intentionally, Michael applies some force upon Terri that renders her unconscious and possibly brings on cardiac arrest.

If that force was a carotid-artery choke hold, and no other blows were delivered, the medical evidence at the autopsy would be virtually indistinguishable from any of the previous scenarios.

WHEN I FIRST DECIDED to write this book, I felt that the one contribution I could make to this case was objectivity, at least as far as the evidence was concerned. I have a great deal of respect for the Schindler family, and am truly sorry for what happened to their daughter. I may not like Michael Schiavo much, but that doesn't mean he killed his wife.

I have no personal investment in any particular conclusion. I simply don't care where the evidence leads. But that doesn't mean I won't push the envelope a little, creating speculative hypotheses in order to try to find out the truth.

One of the above scenarios describes within a certain range of accuracy what happened to Terri Schiavo. I wish I knew which one.

CHAPTER THIRTEEN

The Usual Suspect

When a woman collapses in her home while her husband is present and doctors can't determine the cause, and if she doesn't recover to tell investigators exactly what happened, then the next step is to interview the husband extensively to see if he can shed some light on the case.

If the husband can't get his story right, then he is no longer a witness. Now he's a suspect.

Cops might have more technologically advanced investigative resources at their disposal, but criminals haven't changed. The suspects we are chasing today are no different from the ones my training officers were chasing thirty years ago. They do the same stupid things, lie about the same obvious evidence, and usually talk themselves into jail more often than not. Suspects make mistakes, and they all think they will get away with the crime.

We call them usual suspects. They are not anyone in particular; they change with the dynamics of the case and the environment. Whether the crime is a gang shooting, or a liquor-store robbery, or a residential burglary, we always have our usual suspects.

In situations where women are concerned, the usual suspects are the boyfriends or husbands. I am not implying that every crime against a woman is committed by a husband or boyfriend, or that

Michael Schiavo has any criminal involvement in his wife's collapse, but the husband always needs to be eliminated or included early in the investigation.

This elimination process has no agenda, it's just by-the-numbers detective work. The person who lasts sees the victim is usually the husband. The person who discovers the victim or evidence of her disappearance is usually the husband. The person who shares a home with the victim is usually the husband, and the forensic presence of the husband in the home means almost nothing.

The husband is also the one person who should be able to account for his time, especially the time window when the victim disappeared or died. He is the one person who should have solid and consistent statements. When the people who have the most control over and around the victim begin to change simple and innocent statements, or for some reason can't remember a simple fact, such as the time when they discovered their wife, they become a suspect.

The first seventy-two hours in an investigation are the most crucial. This is true in any murder case, but in domestic homicide, it is even more vital to gather evidence, talk to witnesses, and confront any possible suspects during that narrow window of time. The husband is the most important witness and will be in close and prolonged contact with the responding officers and any detectives who follow. Initially, he will enjoy the sympathy of others. A suspect can take advantage of this to try to hide his crime. While investigators need to be sensitive about questioning someone who has just lost a loved one, they have to keep in mind that their job is to investigate possible criminality, not offer emotional support. You have to look into the eyes of a grieving husband and ask yourself if there is anything to indicate guilt. Sometimes your gut tells you he's dirty. If you're right, then you could be on the way to solving a homicide. If you're wrong, then the evidence will show this, and at least you'll be certain he's clean.

Interviewing a grieving husband or boyfriend, the detective should express empathy while keeping all the possibilities open. Grief can be a crippling mental state, and suspects use this to their advantage. The grieving process, the funeral arrangements and the ceremony itself, the logistics of family coming from out of town—all these contribute to an environment of sympathy, not suspicion. There is confusion, stress, emotional volatility. The challenge to the detective is to try to determine whether these emotions are provoked by genuine grief . . . or fear of being caught.

The suspects in these types of crimes are often middle-class or higher. They have usually never committed even a petty crime, much less murder. But the lack of prior criminal history does not matter to the detective. Domestic murder happens in every type of household and for a variety of different causes or reasons. If the death was an accident, or unintentional, or the result of neglect rather than violence—that's something the suspect knows. It's the detective's job to find out.

A suspect who does not have a criminal history has one significant disadvantage. He does not know how to act, either as a grieving husband or as a murderer. Imagine the conflict in a premeditated murder. He wants his wife dead. He kills her and then has to exhibit grief while being watched by detectives who know the difference between real and fake grief because they have seen both before.

At the same time as the suspect puts on his act, he also has to be careful when describing his actions and observations. Most other suspects do not want to place themselves at the crime scene. This suspect lives there. Most other suspects don't want to have any connection to the victim. This suspect was married to her.

Innocent witnesses don't have to act; the pain of loss comes naturally. It is overwhelming and debilitating. Suspects, on the other hand, shed crocodile tears that an experienced detective should be able to see through.

Remember O. J. Simpson's "suicide note" and the slow-speed pursuit of him and Al Cowlings in the Ford Bronco? What husband whose ex-wife has been murdered wants to kill himself? Why does a grieving ex-husband drive toward the Mexican border with a .357 Magnum, a disguise, and $10,000 in cash?

Or take Scott Peterson. The conduct he displayed in the beginning was not consistent with a husband reporting his wife as a missing person. Normally, when a family member discovers that someone is missing, it takes them some time to come to this conclusion, unless it's a small child. Scott Peterson waited ninety minutes and then called his wife's parents, not just to ask about Laci, but also to establish concern and panic about her absence and, most important, to stop the timeline.

Scott knew that Laci was missing because he had killed her. He thought it would be normal behavior to report her missing as soon as possible. He was also trying to hide his fear of being caught by faking the panic of a husband who believes his wife is missing, even if she has only been gone for an hour and a half. He hoped to mask his guilt with grief. To him it all made sense. To the police officer who took the missing-persons report and the detective who interviewed him hours later, Peterson's act was transparently false.

Peterson's alibi was that he had gone fishing (his alibi placed him in the exact location where his wife's body was eventually found—oops!). He told police that when he left the house, Laci was watching a Martha Stewart program on television, or she was mopping the floor, or she was going to walk the dog. Later investigation determined that the Martha Stewart show he described had been aired the previous day. The first police officer saw a mop and a bucket that had been left out. And the dog was running around loose with a leash on his neck.

When asked what his wife had been doing, Scott would have

been better off saying "I don't know." But suspects often try to answer questions they don't or couldn't know the answers to in order to throw off suspicion. In their guilty minds, they need to account for everything. They think the more they tell the detective, the more the dumb cop is likely to be satisfied, and they will escape suspicion.

The police officer who took the missing-persons report noticed a few details in the husband's story that just didn't seem right: going fishing on Christmas Eve, the fishing tackle that didn't look used, the recently washed clothes Scott Peterson wore that day. The officer called a detective who was three hours away on vacation with his family for Christmas. The officer told him that he didn't think this was a missing-persons case, but a possible homicide. Detective Brochini drove three hours back to Modesto, California, and showed up at Scott Peterson's home. The more questions the detective asked him, the more probable cause Scott created. That probable cause led to search warrants, which led to evidence, which led to Scott's arrest and eventual conviction.

The gut feeling of a cop is the only reason Scott Peterson is on death row today. Had the investigation languished over the holidays or simply fallen through the cracks, Scott Peterson would have had time to dispose of the evidence and get his story straight.

When I was an LAPD detective, there was a case I inherited when I went from robbery to homicide. A husband reported that he had been in bed reading while his wife was in the master bathroom taking a bath. He said he heard a sound from the bathroom, but did not call out to ask what it was or check to see if his wife was okay. After about a half hour, he walked into the master bath and saw his wife in the tub. Her face was under the water and she was not breathing. He called a neighbor who was a doctor and told him his wife was not breathing. When the doctor arrived, he pulled the women from the tub and began CPR. Finally, the husband called 911. It was too late; she was dead.

The case was originally investigated by patrol officers who felt that a detective should take over. A brand-new detective happened to be on call. She was not a homicide detective and did a "routine" investigation before deciding it was an accidental drowning. The detective noted that the victim had petechial hemorrhage in both eyes beneath the lower eyelids, but thought that was consistent with drowning. The medical examiner identified a hematoma to the head as a possible reason for loss of consciousness and possible asphyxia from drowning. The ME and the detective never spoke to compare notes concerning their observations. If they had, they probably would have classified this as a homicide and investigated it further.

Five years later, when I inherited the case, I recognized the accidental drowning as a staged crime scene, where the victim was most probably strangled manually underwater. I reclassified the accidental death to a homicide.

The subsequent investigation was difficult. The husband had remarried and refused to talk. I told his new wife what I believed happened to her predecessor, hoping that might frighten her into telling me what she knew or suspected. She did not cooperate and the case remains unsolved.

The husband's actions were consistent with the behavior of middle-class suspects in domestic homicides. Call someone early to establish urgency, panic, and stop the time. Have them assist at the scene, which is supposedly pristine. Fail to assist the victim.

Detective bureaus all over this country have cases like this. Some of them are eventually solved; many are not. Domestic homicides are usually solved by quick identification of the suspect and his or her immediate commitment to a story. That is why the first seventy-two hours are so important. We can never go back and set the stage again. It is gone forever.

Sometimes the detective has a very small window in which to

recognize, document, and identify evidence. The same narrow time exists for the recognition of suspects and their initial commitment to questions. When a suspect is confronted with prior statements that are contradicted by other evidence, he will either try to offer a different version of his story or take a step on the path to a confession. The only person who usually needs to change his story several times is the suspect.

In these situations, investigating officers are judging everything that is bombarding their senses: body language, speech, emotion, eye contact, and statements. They are following their instincts and at the same time the iron laws of logic and evidence.

The moment when an interview turns to suspicion is electrifying. Your pulse increases ever so slightly and your stomach does a little flip. You keep your eyes unemotional and speech even. You try to control your recognition of a lie.

These are not unusual cases. Some thirteen hundred women will be killed this year by their husbands or boyfriends. Most women and children found murdered in the home are killed by someone they know. This is why the husband, relatives, friends, and other close associations are looked at first and closely to either include them or exclude these possible suspects quickly.

A domestic-homicide case is usually solved by the commitment very early in the investigation of the suspect to a story or remembrance of the events that brings suspicion upon him.

The suspect has two choices. Either he was present with the victim alone and his story describes events that occurred, thereby explaining the injury or death, or he distances himself from the exact time of the incident in question and creates an alibi. The alibi does not need to be very sophisticated, the suspect just needs to not be with the victim at the time of injury, collapse, or attack. The suspect knows where and when he must account for his absence. He knows where he was at the exact moment the victim fell to the floor. The trick is to get him to stumble over his story, which is not based on memory, but on his need to explain things for which he can't innocently account.

What does all this have to do with Terri Schiavo?

Michael Schiavo has not responded to my repeated requests for an interview. So I e-mailed his attorney George Felos the following questions:

> What time did Michael find Terri unconscious in the hall?
>
> Was Michael awake or did the thud wake him?
>
> Did Michael cradle his wife once, twice, three times, or at all?
>
> Why does Michael not acknowledge that he first called Robert Schindler?
>
> Why does Michael constantly state that he called Bobby Schindler that morning and not Robert?
>
> Was Terri breathing or not?
>
> Why does Michael not admit what he and Terri argued about the previous day?
>
> Why can't Michael remember what time he left work and arrived home?
>
> Why didn't Michael help his wife and give her CPR?
>
> How long did Michael wait before he called 911?

If Terri Schiavo had died that morning, or shortly afterward, her case would probably have been handled as a homicide and she would have had a greater chance of receiving justice. The fact that she survived, yet could not communicate for the rest of her life to describe what happened to her, made her incident just another case that fell between the cracks. It wasn't a homicide, there was no evidence of domestic abuse, doctors had a hypothesis for the cause of her collapse, and no one was really pushing for an investigation. So the police simply went through the motions and never really investigated the case.

If Terri had died that morning and a competent detective team had been called in to investigate her death, what can we reasonably expect them to have done?

Police departments the size of the one in St. Petersburg have an "on-call" rotation system for detectives. Upon Terri's death, the officers would have notified their watch commander and informed him that they had a death on their last call and it didn't appear a "natural." The watch commander would have instructed the officers to stand by with the body and witnesses, then he would notify the detective on call.

The initial interviews conducted by the responding officers would either be noted in the officers' notebooks or on an official report. The time the officers arrived, what they observed, and any statements from Michael and Bobby would have been written down. The officers would have looked around the apartment before going to the hospital, where they questioned Michael. Hopefully the officers would have asked Michael when he found his wife unconscious.

The officers' notes would have been passed on to the detective, as well as any other observations, such as their personal read on the players, as we used to say. That's what the cop's gut says to him. How did the scene feel? Was there something that wasn't right, but you just couldn't put your finger on it? How did the husband act? This is the cop-to-cop stuff that courts and the public never hear, but is crucial to getting a read on the case.

Before the detective approached any witnesses, he would get as much medical information as was available at the time. No matter what time he arrived after 7:00 A.M., he would have been told that the victim showed no initial evidence of violence and the cause of death was unknown. This would be a medical examiner's case. Whether it would be deemed a homicide depends on two factors:

one, the autopsy finding of cause of death; and two, the statements of the witness. The medical and witness evidence must be consistent.

Whether he's a crackerjack homicide dick or just a "box checker," the lead detective has to ask the obvious: What time did you find Terri unconscious? Michael had already told emergency-room doctors that morning that he found her at 5:00 A.M. The paramedic run sheet says the 911 call came in at 5:40 A.M. This is a clue.

The detective would approach this situation with the first impression that it most probably involves an as-of-yet-undetermined medical condition and his job is to document the discovery of the victim, record the statements of the witnesses, and answer any questions that might later be asked by the medical examiner.

In his questioning of the direct participants in the victim's collapse, the detective would first try to interview the paramedics and/or fire-department personnel, if they were still at the hospital. These witnesses are professionals, they have documented their actions in notes and later reports, and they are not experiencing the same emotions as those close to the victim. If the paramedics had already left, the detective would start with the witness who first saw the victim. Based on his later statements, Michael would have said that he found the victim unconscious, facedown in the hall/bathroom at some time between 4:30 and 5:00 A.M. He would have described rolling Terri over and cradling her in his arms and calling her name. He would have described calling 911 and either Robert or Bobby Schindler.

This first interview of Michael would have been gentle, even compassionate, for two reasons: There did not appear to be any drugs, domestic violence, or other criminal activity, and this approach would drop the suspect's guard, allowing him to speak freely and commit himself to specific observations concerning the incident. There would be no reason to suspect Michael yet, and the sympathy would come naturally; however, a detective always has to keep in mind the possibility of some criminal involvement.

Once the initial interviews of Michael, Bobby, and Robert had been completed, the detective would have noted some glaring discrepancies. What time did the husband first find her? Whom did he call? Did he and his wife have a fight the day before?

Before the detective reinterviews any parties, he might ask if he could look around the apartment and get a feel for the location where the victim was found. After he gets permission, the detective would tell the husband that he would very much like him to accompany him to the apartment, but he realizes that the husband's place is at the hospital. Michael would have a difficult time refusing the permissive search or accompanying the detective. Detectives know this and play the situation to get permission to search and avoid later legal challenges such as probable cause.

At the apartment, the detective would probably not find anything out of the ordinary, but he would get a feeling for the apartment's spatial dimensions and the location of the victim. He would search the bathroom and look for evidence of urination, defecation, struggle, cleaning, or anything out of place. He would search the bedroom and seen the condition of the bed. Had both sides of the bed been slept in? Were there clothes on the floor? Were both pillows there? Did they have pillowcases?

This is what detectives do just by standing around and looking at a room. It is not a physical search, but a mental one. Notations are made for the next interview of the witnesses, who might not expect to be spoken to again, and certainly won't be prepared for the detective to have considered all of these possibly important details.

As the detective leaves the apartment, he would pick up the phone and press *redial* to see whom the resident last called. According to Michael, it should have been Bobby Schindler.

Returning to the hospital, the detective would once again ask the witnesses for their recollection of the events as best they could remember. First would be Robert Schindler and his wife, Mary. Then Bobby Schindler and finally Michael Schiavo once more. When the detectives evaluated the statements of all the concerned parties, the inconsistencies of Michael's story would become more glaring. The detective would request a private, quiet place to talk. He would ask Michael to repeat what he said about time, phone calls, Terri's body position, and his own actions.

Michael might have an innocent explanation for the discrepancies. This happens all the time. Witnesses bring suspicion on themselves because they lie about something short of criminal involvement. Michael could have felt ashamed that he had panicked and hadn't done more to possibly save Terri's life.

Had Michael stuck to his story, the detective would then confront him with the statements of Bobby and his father-in-law. Michael would have two choices: maintain his version of events or change his story to fit the other witnesses' statements. Not knowing what the detective found or saw at the apartment is a huge advantage to the detective. Only a suspect with something to hide will try to change what innocent witnesses will simply admit was a mistake.

The detective can use deception to draw Michael out. Even if he found nothing in the apartment, Michael doesn't know that. He might be asking himself: Did Terri leave a diary or address book? Is there some evidence he isn't aware of?

This is the opportunity for the detective to get up close and personal with Michael. Let him once again recount the events with all the detail he can muster. The suspect usually tries to add detail to make his story more believable. The detective should maintain eye contact with Michael at every moment and try to see inside him just a little. Is he exhibiting any facial tics? Is he struggling for words? Does he appear more nervous than he'd been earlier that morning? Does he return eye contact?

The truth is easy; lies are hard work.

If the interview turned ugly, that would be entirely up to Michael. Detectives rarely lose the advantage of composure. When they do get angry with an interview subject, it's usually for effect. Had Michael insisted on elements on his story that were contradicted by the evidence or other statements, the detective would elevate the climate of the interview a notch and let Michael know that he thought he was lying about several issues. Michael would need to explain these problems . . . or become a suspect.

The detective could give Michael an out—an escape hatch is what I used to call it. Provide him with a place to go: Are you protecting someone else? Are you embarrassed by your failure to perform CPR, I understand, talk to me . . . it will just be man-to-man.

Now is the time to play yo-yo with the suspect. The detective leaves him alone for a few minutes. When he returns, the detective apologizes for the accusation and sympathizes with his situation. He asks Michael to tell his whole story, no matter what it is.

The detective buys time, meanwhile planning to use Michael's statements to obtain a search warrant for the apartment and phone records.

On Monday the detective attends the victim's autopsy. The cause of death might be determined as natural causes, but if it is ruled unknown, the investigation continues.

The detective contacts friends and family members looking for recent disturbances or unusual conduct of the victim, any fears or complaints that she expressed. Terri's best friend and coworker would say that Terri had a fight with Michael that Saturday over her hair. Jackie would go on to tell the detective that Terri wanted a divorce and she and Terri had begun planning to get an apartment together. Jackie would also add that Terri and a UPS driver were quite friendly at work and Terri had gone to lunch with him on several occasions. These lunch dates were right before Terri collapsed.

The detective would visit Agostino's restaurant and find out exactly what time Michael Schiavo left work that Saturday night. He would talk to coworkers to see if Michael went out for drinks with them, or if he was particularly close to any of the female staff.

The next interview would be at the police station, using a ruse that the detective needs to ask Michael a couple more questions so he can close out the investigation. Michael would respond and be confronted with not one detective but two—who might not be so empathetic today.

The interview would quickly shift to interrogation. The detectives would demand that Michael clear up the inconsistencies in his statements.

If they still thought he was lying, the detectives would ask Michael to take a polygraph test. If he declined and lawyered up, the case would now be in limbo.

That's one possibility. Here's another: I believe Michael Schiavo has such a volatile temper that he could not withstand the intensity of an interrogation or the lack of control he would feel during one. He would confess to whatever really did happen, and the case would be closed within twenty-four hours.

Why does someone have to die before a thorough investigation is performed? If this had been done fifteen years ago, we wouldn't have so many questions today. And Terri Schiavo might still be alive.

CHAPTER FOURTEEN

Statute of Limitations

Homicide: The killing of another by one's act or omission.

The state of Florida committed a legal homicide upon Terri Schiavo. They did it on the direction of Michael Schiavo, following his wishes. While he often said he was doing this for Terri, it was always all about him.

But that doesn't mean he's the only one to blame.

After someone dies, people often say they would have liked to help, but now it's too late. If only they had known . . .

That first day, paramedics and doctors were too busy saving Terri's life to determine what had caused her collapse in the first place. Afterward, they left the question unanswered.

The police investigation was shamefully incomplete.

Terri's family was too innocent in their own hearts to suspect foul play. When Robert Schindler was asked whether he thought Michael could have had something to do with it, he said, "No. No way." He is a loving father and a good man who tries to see the good in people. He forgot about the misgivings he had about Michael because he couldn't imagine his son-in-law hurting his daughter.

Terri's brother and sister had their own ideas about Michael, but they didn't say anything, not wanting to upset their parents. Some of Terri's closest friends had asked her if she was sure she wanted to marry Michael. When they didn't like what they saw, they hoped that Michael would change and love Terri as they did.

Terri spent fifteen years in a series of health-care facilities where she was seen and treated by hundreds of nurses, administrators, and orderlies. Why have only a handful of nurses come forward to describe the abuse and neglect she suffered at the hands of Michael Schiavo? The fact that these nurses worked in separate facilities and yet saw the same behavior is powerful corroborative evidence. I wouldn't be surprised if many more caregivers saw things, but said nothing because they were afraid of reprisals, or did not want to violate their confidentiality oaths. When Terri was suffering her prolonged and very public death, why didn't they come forward? How many other nurses had intimate relationships with Michael Schiavo and are embarrassed to admit it?

Judge George Greer consistently ruled in Michael Schiavo's favor. When he heard testimony of Michael, Scott, and Joan Schiavo concerning Terri's end-of-life wishes, he pronounced it "clear and convincing." Presented with evidence that testimony was perjured, Greer said it was too late.

All the judges who reviewed the case could have done something, but they didn't want to overrule one of their brethren and so they let the original decisions stand. Terri was not afforded the constitutional protections given to death-row inmates awaiting execution.

After Jay Wolfson's ad litum report, the Schindlers asked that he be removed because of evident bias. I agree with them. To read Wolfson's report for yourself, log on to this web page: http://www.miami.edu/ethics/schiavo/wolfson%27s%20report.pdf

Jeb Bush, George Bush, the Florida state legislature, and the United States Congress tried to help, but did so in such a clumsy manner that their efforts were ruled unconstitutional and found repulsive by an overwhelming majority of Americans.

The news media ignored many of the Schindlers' sworn and corroborated charges of Michael's abuse and neglect, choosing to see the case as a conflict between the "right-to-life" and "right-to-die" movements, and often siding with the latter.

The Pinellas County Sheriff's Department, Florida State Attorney's Office, and Florida Department of Children and Families all refused to investigate the charges of abuse and neglect. On June 3, 2003, Robert Schindler asked the office of the Florida state attorney to open an investigation based upon evidence of Michael Schiavo's possible domestic abuse, his perjured testimony and fraud on the court stemming from the medical malpractice trial, and his alleged misuse of Terri's medical trust fund.

Nine days later, Robert got a call from Assistant State Attorney Robert Lewis, who told him there were no crimes to investigate. Lewis stated that he had read Michael's transcripts, and even though Michael had promised to take care of Terri in the future, he had the right to change his mind. Concerning the financial records, Lewis said that since Terri's bills were being paid, there was no reason to investigate further. Finally, he said that any alleged perjury or physical abuse was beyond the statute of limitations.

On August 6, 2003, Robert Schindler called the St. Petersburg police and asked them to investigate the possibility that Michael had caused Terri's collapse. He was told that the department would not investigate the charges, or even take a report. Two days later Robert called again, this time speaking with a different officer, who took a formal complaint charging that Michael had caused Terri's collapse and heart failure. That officer advised Robert that the information would be passed on and assigned to a detective. As of press time, there has been no follow-up.

Everyone failed Terri. The people charged with her care disconnected her feeding tube and then stood aside and watched her die. The police sworn to protect and serve her arrested protesters outside the hospice while she starved to death. The politicians so dedicated to her plight turned tail and ran once the poll numbers went against them. The judges sworn to uphold the law allowed her to be killed by due process.

In order for evil to prosper, it is only necessary that good men do nothing.

This is exactly what happened in the case of Terri Schiavo.

Even I stood on the sidelines, without knowing I had the opportunity to help. Speaking with the Schindlers' lawyers, I learned that they had tried to contact me through my radio station the second time Terri's feeding tube had been removed. I receive a lot of requests to investigate cases, and honestly don't remember getting the message. If I had gotten involved, perhaps I would have been able to make a difference. But I didn't, and for that I am deeply sorry.

There are statutes of limitations for every crime except murder. Other crimes are given a period of time during which they can be investigated and prosecuted. No matter how heinous or vicious, those crimes must be solved within three to seven years. After that, the slate is wiped clean and the suspect has nothing to worry about.

Yet we find murder so unforgivable, and repugnant, that we leave the case open until it is solved, as if someone must speak for the dead.

If Michael Schiavo is a suspect in his wife's collapse, he has only himself to blame. Here we have a case that might not even be a crime, but the husband's statements are so inconsistent regarding the questions of how and when Terri collapsed that he brings suspicion upon himself. Certainly his behavior after the medical malpractice award makes him appear even worse. Why was he so determined that Terri Schiavo not get therapy? Was he afraid she might recover enough to talk?

Michael spent a lot of time, and a lot of Terri's money, pursuing all the various legal procedures to have her feeding tube removed. Since 1993, the Schindler family offered to take complete responsibility for her. In 2005, they offered him a million dollars to divorce her, give up the guardianship, and allow them to care for her. He refused.

If all Michael Schiavo wanted was to get on with his life, he could have done so without having Terri die. Why was it so important to him? And why, when he testified in 1993 about a doctor's suggestion that he withdraw her feeding tube, did he say, "I could never do that for Terri"? Why, when he testified in 1992, did he promise to take care of her for as long as he lived? Did he change his mind about her, or had she already served his purposes? Were there other life-insurance policies that he cashed in on? Or was he motivated by some darker, more twisted motive to end Terri's life?

Only Michael Schiavo knows the answer to these questions.

I would have liked to interrogate him on the morning of February 2, 1990. I would have liked some competent police officer to have interrogated him at that time.

"If we could ever depose Michael Schiavo, it would be over," Pat Anderson, a Schindler family attorney, told me. Every time Pat has subpoenaed him, Michael found some reason not to appear.

And every previous time that Michael has recounted the events of February 25, 1990, he gives a different story. I'd like to know the truth. And I have a feeling I'm not the only one. If we are ever to determine what happened to Terri Schiavo, we need more than just medical evidence. We need to find out what happened that morning.

There were two witnesses to Terri Schiavo's collapse.

One of them died without telling her story.

The other is still alive.

If Terri Schiavo had recovered her speech enough to describe the events leading to her collapse, she might have been able to clear up this mystery. Medical opinion was divided on the question of whether or not she had been able to recover to the point of being able to communicate again. There is also the possibility that her brain damage would keep her from even remembering what happened. Now that she's dead, these issues are moot.

With Terri Schiavo's death, the mystery surrounding her collapse has been elevated to a suspicious death, possibly even a homicide. There is one person who can solve this mystery with a complete, accurate, and truthful statement concerning the events of the early morning of February 25, 1990. Michael Schiavo has already cast suspicion on himself through a series of conflicting and problematic statements. If he does not wish to speak any further on this subject, he can be compelled to do so by a grand jury or special prosecutor investigation.

Florida governor Jeb Bush has the statutory authority to call for a special prosecutor. His brother the president can order an investigation by the Department of Justice. Both of them were very active in trying to save Terri Schiavo's life, up to a certain point. Whether their final decisions not to intervene in the case were motivated by respect for the separation of powers or fear of opinion polls is something only they know for certain. Many people say George and Jeb Bush let Terri Schiavo down. Now it may be too late to save her life, but they can still do something to solve the mystery surrounding her death.

Called before a grand jury, Michael would be asked to tell his story once again. This time, an experienced criminal prosecutor would not allow him to get away with the memory lapses and inconsistencies that have made his prior statements so problematic.

Michael would have the right to take the Fifth. And if he did, that would be a pretty good indication to me he's got something to hide.

Here's what I think it is.

Terri Schiavo was fed up. She had suffered Michael's control and abuse for six years of marriage, and now she realized she didn't have to take it any longer. She was at an emotional crossroads. A practicing Catholic who had married the first man she had ever dated, Terri now faced the anguish of telling her parents that she wanted a divorce. Two weeks prior to her collapse, Terri broke down in tears and told her brother she couldn't take being married to Michael and wished she had the guts to divorce him.

Terri had grown up. She was letting go of her childhood and its dreams of innocence. Another man was taking her to lunch and entertaining her with respect and humor and attention. Terri was ready to move on.

We know that Terri and Michael had a fight the day before her collapse. Michael talked his way around that inconvenient fact when speaking to the police.

I would find this highly coincidental. If I believed in coincidences.

This story plays out every day in America. A relationship goes sideways and people turn ugly. There's rage, threats, stalking, 911 calls, restraining orders, court proceedings. Sometimes there's violence. Sometimes it ends in death. When it does, we call it murder. If we recognize it as such.

There are larger lessons in this case, but they're not about living wills or the debate over euthanasia. At least not for me. I'm worried about the other Terri Schiavos out there, the ones we never hear about. The women who die at the hands of their husbands or boyfriends, the cases that never make the newspaper and no one ever investigates. How many women have died? How many men have gotten away with murder?

Whatever happened to Terri Schiavo, she lived with it for fifteen years, a silent witness to the truth. Then, since she was unable to speak for herself, Michael Schiavo spoke for her. He said she wanted to die.

Who will speak for Terri Schiavo now?

Appendix A: Timeline

December 3, 1963
Theresa Marie Schindler born.

November 10, 1984
Terri marries Michael Schiavo.

February 25, 1990
Terri suffers cardiorespiratory arrest. She is taken to the Humana
Northside Hospital.

May 9, 1990
Terri discharged from the hospital and taken to the College
Harbor nursing home.

June 18, 1990
Court appoints Michael Schiavo as guardian. Terri's parents are
not informed of hearing.

June 30, 1990
Terri transferred to Bayfront Hospital.

September 1990

Family brings Terri home. Three weeks later they return her to College Park facility "overwhelmed by care needs."

November 29, 1990, to January 20, 1991

Michael takes Terri to California for experimental brain stimulator treatment.

January 1991

Terri placed in Mediplex Rehabilitation Center in Bradenton.

February 22, 1991

Terri expresses signs of pain during physical therapy. Bone scan ordered.

March 5, 1991

Bone scan and report.

March 26, 1991

Side rail on Terri's bed found down after a visit by Michael. When told about it, he replies, "That was their job."

July 19, 1991

Terri is transferred to Sabel Palms nursing home.

May 1992

Michael moves out of Schindlers' house. After this, he euthanizes Terri's cats and turns her engagement ring and wedding band into jewelry for himself.

August 1992

Terri is awarded $250,000 in out-of-court settlement for medical malpractice suit.

November 10, 1992
Jury in medical malpractice trial awards Terri close to $1 million.
Michael receives $400,000 for loss of consortium.

November 10, 1992
Michael and Cindy Brashers break up. Michael and Trudy
Capone end their relationship.

February 14, 1993
Michael and Schindlers fight over the use of the malpractice
award.

February 14, 1993
Michael posts "do not resuscitate" order in Terri's medical chart.

August 1993
Michael orders medical staff not to treat Terri for sepsis.

July 29, 1993
Schindlers attempt to remove Michael Schiavo as guardian.
Court eventually dismisses the suit.

March 1, 1994
John Pecarek, first guardian ad litem, submits report saying
Michael has acted appropriately toward Terri.

September 1995
Michael orders Palm Gardens staff not to treat Terri for
potentially fatal infection.

July 1997
Michael's engagement to Jodi Centonze announced in obituary of
Claire Schiavo.

August 1997
George Felos sends Schindlers letter notifying them of action to remove feeding tube.

May 1998
Michael Schiavo petitions court to authorize removal of Terri's feeding tube.

October 1998
Michael offers to donate Terri's estate to charity if family allows him to remove feeding tube.

December 20, 1998
Second guardian ad litem Richard Pearse issues report recommending the court not approve Michael's request to remove feeding tube.

January 24, 2000
Trial before county circuit-court judge George Greer to determine whether or not Terri's feeding tube should be removed.

February 11, 2000
Judge Greer rules that, based on comments she allegedly made to Michael, his brother, and his sister-in-law, Terri would have wanted her feeding tube removed. He orders it removed.

March 3, 2000
Terri admitted to Hospice Woodside. Certified as terminally ill with less than six months to live.

March 12, 2001
Michael petitions to have feeding tube removed immediately.

March 29, 2001
Judge Greer orders feeding tube removed.

April 12, 2001
Schindlers file motion requesting that Greer recuse himself.

April 16, 2001
Greer denies the Schindlers' motion.

April 24, 2001
Terri's feeding tube is removed.

April 25, 2001
Cindy Brashers Shook appears on local radio talking about her relationship with Michael Schiavo.

April 26, 2001
The Schindlers file an emergency motion with Judge Greer based on new evidence. Greer dismisses the motion. The Schindlers follow with civil suit claiming Michael perjured himself in January 24, 2000, trial. Circuit judge Frank Quesada orders feeding tube reinserted.

August 7, 2001
Greer orders feeding tube removed.

August 17, 2001
Greer delays removal of Terri's feeding tube until October 9 in order to allow the Schindlers time to appeal.

October 3, 2001
Second District Court of Appeals delays removal of Terri's feeding tube indefinitely.

October 17, 2001
Second District Court of Appeals rules that five doctors should examine Terri to determine if she can improve with new medical treatment.

November 16, 2001
Terri's medical testing plan to be determined before mediator.

December 19, 2001
Attorneys meet with a mediator to determine which tests doctors should run.

February 13, 2002
Mediation fails.

October 2002
Michael Schiavo petitions Judge Greer to have Terri cremated after her death.

November 15, 2002
Greer conducts hearing to investigate evidence that Terri's collapse might have been caused by physical abuse.

November 22, 2002
Greer orders that Terri's feeding tube be removed January 3, 2003.

August 15, 2003
Terri hospitalized for sepsis.

August 24, 2003
Terri hospitalized again for sepsis.

August 29, 2003
Terri hospitalized a third time for sepsis.

August 25, 2003
Michael petitions court for authority to deny treatment of sepsis.

August 30, 2003
The Schindlers file a federal lawsuit challenging the removal of Terri's feeding tube.

September 17, 2003
Greer orders the removal of Terri's feeding tube on October 15, 2003.

October 15, 2003
Terri's feeding tube removed again.

October 20, 2003
Florida House of Representatives passes Terri's Law.

October 21, 2003
Florida Senate passes Terri's Law. Governor Bush issues an executive order directing reinsertion of the feeding tube and appointing a guardian ad litem.

October 21, 2003
Terri's feeding tube is reinserted. Michael announces plans to sue Governor Bush and challenge Terri's Law as unconstitutional.

October 28, 2003
President George Bush praises the way his brother has handled the Schiavo case.

October 31, 2003
Dr. Jay Wolfson appointed guardian ad litem.

December 1, 2003
Wolfson concludes that Terri is in a persistent vegetative state with no chance of improvement.

March 20, 2004
In a direct reference to Terri's case, Pope John Paul II says providing food and water is not medical treatment.

March 29, 2004
Nursing home workers observe a puncture on Terri's arms shortly after visit by the Schindlers. Blood screen and police investigation clear the Schindlers.

September 23, 2004
Florida Supreme Court unanimously declares Terri's Law unconstitutional.

October 22, 2004
Greer stays the removal of Terri's feeding tube until December 6, 2004.

January 10, 2005
The Schindlers ask Greer to remove Michael Schiavo as guardian.

January 24, 2005
U.S. Supreme Court refuses to grant a review of the case in which the Florida Supreme Court struck down Terri's Law as unconstitutional.

February 25, 2005
Greer orders that Terri's feeding tube be removed on March 18.

March 10, 2005
Judge Greer denies Florida's Department of Children and
Families the right to intervene in the case.

March 17, 2005
Florida House of Representatives approves H.701, meant to
prevent the suspension of medically supplied nutrition and
hydration. Florida Senate votes down S.804, a similar bill.

March 18, 2005
Terri's feeding tube is removed. The U.S. House of Representatives
Committee on Government Reform issues subpoenas to Terri and
Michael Schiavo as well as hospice workers.

March 19–20, 2005
Delaying Easter recess, the U.S. Senate passes bill meant to keep
Terri alive. The U.S. House of Representatives returns from
Easter recess to debate the bill.

March 21, 2005
The House votes 203–58 to pass the bill. President Bush signs it
into law.

March 24, 2005
The U.S. Supreme Court refuses to hear the Schindlers' case.

March 27, 2005
Governor Bush refuses to take Terri under protective custody,
saying that he cannot violate a court order.

March 30, 2005

The Eleventh Circuit Court denies the Schindlers' motion for rehearing. The U.S. Supreme Court refuses to review the Eleventh Circuit Court ruling, exhausting the Schindlers' legal options.

March 31, 2005

Terri Schiavo dies at 9:05 A.M.

Appendix B

Report Title: CALL FOR ASSISTANCE
Occurred: SUN 02/25/1990 05:40   To:
Call Received:
Dispatched: 02/25/1990 06:11   Arrived: 06:33   Completed: 08:55
Incident Address.: 12201 9 ST N   Apt/Unit: 2210
City.:ST PETERSBURG   State: FLORIDA   Zip: 33716
Census Tract: 0462   Zone: 23   Dist: 2   Area:

---------------------------------- PERSONS ----------------------------------

Relationship: WITNESS   Type: OTHER
Name.: SCHIAVO, THERESA MARIE   W/F Dob: 12/03/1963 Age: 39 Aprx Age: 26
Occupation: FIELD SERVICE REP.
Address: 12201 9 ST N   Apt/Unit: 2210 City: ST PETERSBURG
State: FLORIDA   Zip: 33716   Home Phone: 813-577-0012
Employer: PRUDENTIAL INS./SEMINOLE   Work Phone: 813-391-2410
Synopsis:

Relationship: WITNESS   Type: OTHER
Name.: SCHIAVO, MICHAEL RICHARD   W/M Dob: 04/03/1963 Age: 40 Aprx Age: 26
Occupation: GENERAL MANAGER
Address: 12201 9 ST N   Apt/Unit: 2210 City: ST PETERSBURG
State: FLORIDA   Zip: 33716   Home Phone: 813-577-0012
Employer: AGOSTINOS RISTORANTE/CLRWTR Work Phone: 813-573-2040
Synopsis: FOUND WIFE UNCONSCIOUS ON FLOOR/CALLED PARAMEDICS

---------------------------------- EVIDENCE ----------------------------------

Processed: NO   By: Photos: NO   Prints: NO

-------------------------------- ADMINISTRATION --------------------------------

Officer1: BREWER, PHILLIP R   #: 24914 Unit: Date: 02/25/1990
Officer2: TOWER, RODNEY L   #: 28194 Unit:
-Route...: HOMICIDE
Sac.....: N/A   Date: Division:
Clearance: Exception: Cl. Date: 02/25/1990
Supervisor: CHAPMAN, GEORGE B   RET #:11657
Approved By: #:24914
Attachments: NONE

---------------------------------- NARRATIVE ----------------------------------

**** This investigation was originally conducted by myself and
then-probationary officer Rodney Tower. The date of the investigation was
February 25, 1990. The report was typed and uploaded into the Police
Information computer system by me at the end of that shift. The report was
transferred to microfilm some time ago and is no longer stored in P.I.

ST. PETERSBURG POLICE DEPARTMENT   90-024846

Similarly, no entry exists in the P.I. system that this report was ever
generated or uploaded. The quality of the microfilm onto which the report was
transferred has degenerated; the report can be read on the microfilm screen
but it is largely unreadable in printed form. Due to the circumstances of
this case, I have reproduced the report in its entirety so the record can be
preserved. This new entry is absolutely accurate as to the content of the
narrative, which could be easily read on the microfilm screen. The captions
are also easily readable on the microfilm screen and they, too, were
reproduced accurately as to content. Only small, technical aspects of the
captions are different because the report writing format has changed since
1990. The date and times listed in the first and last captions reflect the
date and times recorded during the original investigation, not the date and
times this report was reproduced, which was Wednesday, October 22, 2003.
Below is the narrative as it was written on February 25, 1990. ****

===

WRITER RESPONDED TO THE ABOVE ADDRESS IN REFERENCE TO PARAMEDICS NEEDING
ASSISTANCE ON A MEDICAL EMERGENCY.

UPON ARRIVAL, WRITER SPOKE WITH FIREFIGHTER/PARAMEDIC J. RADJESKI. HE STATED
HE RESPONDED TO THE ADDRESS FOR A MEDICAL EMERGENCY. THEY FOUND A SUBJECT IN
QUESTION (THERESA) LYING FACE DOWN AND UNCONSCIOUS HALFWAY IN AND HALFWAY OUT
OF A BATHROOM. SHE WAS UNRESPONSIVE THE ENTIRE TIME AND WAS TRANSPORTED TO
HUMANA NORTHSIDE HOSPITAL BY SUNSTAR MEDIC ONE AMBULANCE #328 (J. CAMPBELL AND
J. EISENBRANDT). SHE WAS FOUND WITH HER HEAD FACING EAST OUT INTO A HALLWAY
AND HER FEET AND LEGS POINTING WEST ON THE BATHROOM FLOOR. HE STATED SHE
SHOWED NO OUTWARD SIGNS OF VIOLENCE. THE POLICE WERE CALLED BECAUSE OF HER
AGE AND BECAUSE THE SITUATION SEEMED UNUSUAL.

WRITER FOUND NOTHING UNUSUAL INSIDE THE APARTMENT. THERE WERE NO SIGNS OF A
STRUGGLE OR ANYTHING THAT WOULD INDICATE A CRIME HAD BEEN COMMITTED. VARIOUS
BOTTLES OF PRESCRIPTION MEDICATION WERE PRESENT IN THE KITCHEN; HOWEVER, ONLY
TWO WERE PRESCRIBED TO THERESA.

WRITER SECURED THE APARTMENT AND BROUGHT THE KEYS TO THE HOSPITAL. WRITER
SPOKE WITH THERESA'S HUSBAND (MICHAEL) WHO STATED HE WAS AWAKENED THIS MORNING
WHEN HE HEARD A THUD. HE THOUGHT HIS WIFE HAD FALLEN DOWN AND GOT UP TO CHECK
ON HER. HE FOUND HER UNCONSCIOUS ON THE FLOOR AND CALLED PARAMEDICS.

MICHAEL STATED HE DOESN'T KNOW WHAT COULD BE WRONG WITH THERESA. THERE
HAVEN'T BEEN ANY PROBLEMS AT HOME WHICH WOULD LEAD TO HER WANTING TO TRY
SUICIDE AND THEY HAVE HAD NO MAJOR ARGUMENTS LATELY. SHE IS ALLERGIC TO
CERTAIN ITEMS BUT KNOWS WHAT NOT TO INGEST. SHE DOESN'T HAVE A HISTORY OF
HEART DISEASE. SHE HAS HAD RECENT "FEMALE" PROBLEMS AND IS SEEING HER
GYNECOLOGIST ON A REGULAR BASIS. SHE HAS BEEN TIRED LATELY AND NOT FEELING
WELL.

WHEN WRITER OBSERVED THERESA SHE WAS STILL UNCONSCIOUS AND ON A RESPIRATOR.
MEDICAL PERSONNEL ADVISED THAT SHE WAS UNRESPONSIVE UPON ARRIVAL. A DRUG
SCREEN REVEALED NO AMOUNTS OF ILLEGAL NARCOTICS PRESENT IN HER SYSTEM AND HER
BLOOD ALCOHOL LEVEL MEASURED AT "LESS THAN 10", WHICH A NURSE DESCRIBED AS
BEING THE BOTTOM OF THE SCALE. A PHYSICAL INSPECTION BY WRITER ALSO REVEALED

ST. PETERSBURG POLICE DEPARTMENT   PAGE 2

ST. PETERSBURG POLICE DEPARTMENT 90-024846

NO SIGNS OF TRAUMA TO HER HEAD OR FACE.

WRITER REMAINED AT THE HOSPITAL FOR THE OUTCOME OF THE CAT SCAN. THE SCAN REVEALED NO "MID-LINE SHIFT" OF THE BRAIN WHICH WOULD INDICATE AN OBVIOUS ABNORMALITY. ADDITIONAL TESTING IS NECESSARY TO DETECT A POSSIBLE ANEURYSM OR PULMONARY EMBOLISM.

WRITER GAVE MICHAEL A BUSINESS CARD WITH THE OFFENSE NUMBER. HE WAS TOLD THAT WRITER WOULD CALL FOR AN UPDATE OF HER CONDITION AND NO FURTHER ACTION WAS TAKEN.

EOR

ST. PETERSBURG POLICE DEPARTMENT   PAGE 3

BOBBY SCHINDLER DIAGRAM

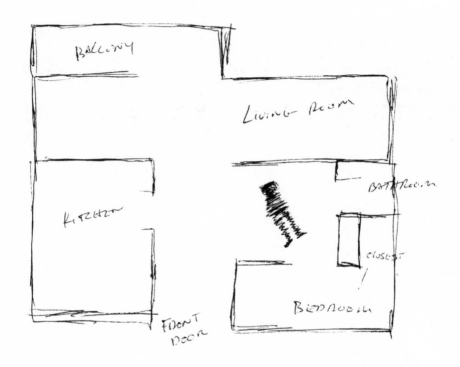

BONE SCAN

NUCLEAR IMAGING

3/5/91

MAR 0 7 1991

BONE SCAN:
Indication: Evaluate for trauma.

Procedure and findings: Multiple gamma camera images of the
axial and proximal appendicular skeleton in the anterior and
posterior projections were obtained, following 21.1
millicuries of Technetium 99m HDP. There are an extensive
number of focal abnormal areas of nuclide accumulation of
intense type. These include, multiple bilateral ribs, the
costovertebral aspects of several of the thoracic vertebral
bodies, the L1 vertebral body, both sacroiliac joints, the
distal right femoral diaphysis, both knees, and both ankles,
right greater than left. Correlative radiographs are
obtained of the lumbar spine and of the right femur which
reveal compression fracture, minor, superior end plate of L1
and shaggy irregular periosteal ossification along the
distal femoral diaphysis and metaphysis primarily
ventrally. The patient has a history of trauma, most
likely the femoral periosteal reaction reflects a response
to a subperiosteal hemorrhage and the activity in L1
correlates perfectly with the compression fracture which is
presumably traumatic. The presumption is that the other
multiple areas of abnormal activity also relate to previous
trauma. Additional possibility would be neoplastic bone
disease, widespread disseminated infectious bone disease or
multiple bone infarcts from abnormal hemoglobin.

CONCLUSION
Multiple areas of abnormal scintigraphic accumulation some
of which are radiograph for differential as discussed
above.

W. CAMPBELL WALKER, M.D./mjt
Dictated 3/5/91
Transcribed 3/5/91

TEE MEMORIAL HOSPITAL
RADIOLOGY DEPARTMENT

SIGNATURE OF RADIOLOGIST

Appendix C

AFFIDAVIT

STATE OF FLORIDA
COUNTY OF PINELLAS

BEFORE ME the undersigned authority personally appeared HEIDI LAW who

being first duly sworn deposes and says:

1. My name is Heidi Law, I am over the age of 18 years, and make this
    statement on personal information.

2. I worked as a Certified Nursing Assistant at the Palm Gardens nursing
    home from March, 1997 to mid-summer of 1997. While I was employed at
    Palm Gardens, occasionally I took care of Theresa Schiavo. Generally, I
    worked the 3 p.m. to 11 p.m. shift, but occasionally also would work a
    double shift, until 7 a.m. the following morning.

3. At Palm Gardens, most of the patient care was provided by the CNAs, so I
    was in a good position to judge Terri's condition and observe her reactions.
    Terri was noticeable, because she was the youngest patient at Palm
    Gardens.

4. I know that Terri did not receive routine physical therapy or any other kind
    of therapy. I was personally aware of orders for rehabilitation that were not
    being carried out. Even though they were ordered, Michael would stop
    them. Michael ordered that Terri receive no rehabilitation or range of

motion therapy. I and Olga would give Terri range of motion anyway, but we knew we were endangering our jobs by doing so. We usually did this behind closed doors, we were so fearful of being caught. Our hearts would race and we were always looking out for Michael, because we knew that, not only would Michael take his anger out on us, but he would take it out more on Terri. We spoke of this many times.

5. Terri had very definite likes and dislikes. Olga and I used to call Terri "Fancy Pants," because she was so particular about certain things. She just adored her baths, and was so happy afterward when she was all clean, smelling sweet from the lotion her mother provided, and wearing the soft nightgowns her mother laundered for her. Terri definitely did not like the taste of the teeth-cleaning swabs or the mouthwash we used. She liked to have her hair combed. She did not like being tucked in, and especially hated it if her legs were tightly tucked. You would always tell when Terri had a bowel movement, as she seem agitated and would sort of "scoot" to get away from it.

6. Every day, Terri was gotten up after lunch and sat in a chair all afternoon. When Terri was in bed, she very much preferred to lie on her right side and look out the window. We always said that she was watching for her mother. It was very obvious that her mother was her favorite person in the

whole world.

7.   I worked side-by-side with another CNA named Olga and could tell that she
     and Terri were especially close. Olga took a definite personal interest in
     Terri, and Terri responded to her. I could tell that Terri was very satisfied
     and happy with Olga's attentions to her.

8.   When Olga was talking with Terri, Terri would follow Olga with her eyes.
     I have no doubt in my mind that Terri understood what Olga was saying to
     her. I could tell a definite difference between the way Terri responded to
     Olga and the way she reacted to me, until she got used to my taking care of
     her. Initially, she "clammed up" with me, the way she would with anyone
     she did not know or was not familiar or comfortable with. It took about the
     fourth or fifth time taking care of her alone, without Olga, that Terri became
     relaxed and cooperative and non-resistant with me.

9.   Terri reacted very well to seeing a picture of her mother, which was in her
     room. Many times when I came on duty it would be lying face down where
     she could not see it.

10. At least three times during any shift where I took care of Terri, I made sure
     to give Terri a wet washcloth filled with ice chips, to keep her mouth
     moistened. I personally saw her swallow the ice water and never saw her
     gag. Olga and I frequently put orange juice or apple juice in her washcloth

to give her something nice to taste, which made her happy. On three or four occasions I personally fed Terri small mouthfuls of Jello, which she was able to swallow and enjoyed immensely. I did not do it more often only because I was so afraid of being caught by Michael.

11. On one occasion Michael Schiavo arrived with his girlfriend, and they entered Terri's room together. I heard Michael tell his girlfriend that Terri was in a persistent vegetative state and was dying. After they left, Olga told me that Terri was extremely agitated and upset, and wouldn't react to anyone. When she was upset, which was usually the case after Michael was there, she would withdraw for hours. We were convinced that he was abusing her, and probably saying cruel, terrible things to her because she would be so upset when he left.

12. In the past, I have taken care of comatose patients, including those in a persistent vegetative state. While it is true that those patients will flinch or make sounds occasionally, they don't do it as a reaction to someone on a constant basis who is taking care of them, the way I saw Terri do.

13. I witnessed a priest visiting Terri a couple of times. Terri would become quiet when he prayed with her. She couldn't bow her head because of her stiff neck, but she would still try. During the prayer, she would keep her eyes closed, opening them afterward. She laughed at jokes he told her. I

definitely know that Terri "is in there."

14.   The Palm Gardens staff, myself included, were just amazed that a "Do Not Resuscitate" order had been put on Terri's chart, considering her age and her obvious cognitive awareness of her surroundings.

15.   During the time I cared for Terri, she formed words. I have heard her say "mommy" from time to time, and "momma," and she also said "help me" a number of times. She would frequently make noises like she was trying to talk. Other staff members talked about her verbalizations.

16.   Several times when Michael visited Terri during my shift, he went into her room alone and closed the door. This worried me because I didn't trust Michael. When he left, Terri was very agitated, was extremely tense with tightened fists and some times had a cold sweat. She was much less responsive than usual and would just stare out the window, her eyes kind of glassy. It would take much more time and effort than usual to work her hands open to clean her palms.

17.   I was told by supervisory staff that Michael was Terri's legal guardian, and that it didn't matter what the parents or the doctors or nurses wanted, just do what Michael told you to do or you will lose your job. Michael would override the orders of the doctors and nurses to make sure Terri got no treatment. Among the things that Terri was deprived of by Michael's orders

were any kind of testing, dental care or stimulation. I was ordered by my supervisors to limit my time with Terri. I recall telling my supervisor that Terri seemed abnormally warm to the touch. I was told to pull her covers down, rather than to take her temperature. As far as I know, Terri never left her room. The only stimulation she had was looking out the window and watching things, and the radio, which Michael insisted be left on one particular station. She had a television, and there was a sign below it saying not to change the channel. This was because of Michael's orders.

18. As a CNA, I wanted every piece of information I could get about my patients. I never had access to medical records as a CNA, but it was part of my job duties to write my observations down on sheets of paper, which I turned over to the nurse at the nurses station for inclusion in the patients charts. In the case of Terri Schiavo, I felt that my notes were thrown out without even being read. There were trash cans at the nurses stations that we were supposed to empty each shift, and I often saw the notes in them. I made extensive notes and listed all of Terri's behaviors, but there was never any apparent follow up consistent with her responsiveness.

19. I discussed this situation with other personnel at Palm Gardens, particularly with Olga, and another CNA, an older black man named Ewan Morris. We all discussed the fact that we could be fired for reporting that Terri was

responsive, and especially for giving her treatment. The advice among the staff was "don't do nothin', don't see nothin' and don't say nothin'." It was particularly distressing that we always had to be afraid that if Michael got upset, he would take his anger out on Terri.

20.   I recall an incident when Olga became very upset because Terri started to get a sore spot, because it might lead to a bedsore. Michael was told about it but didn't seem to care. He didn't complain about it all, in fact, saying "she doesn't know the difference." When Terri would get a UTI or was sick, Michael's mood would improve.

FURTHER AFFIANT SAYETH NAUGHT.

                                                        Heidi Law, Affiant

STATE OF FLORIDA
COUNTY OF PINELLAS

Sworn to and subscribed before me this ___ day of September, 2003, by HEIDI LAW, who produced a Florida Driver's License as identification.

Notary Public

My Commission expires:

Thomas A. Brodersen
MY COMMISSION # DD189485 EXPIRES
March 4, 2007
BONDED THRU TROY FAIN INSURANCE, INC.

AFFIDAVIT

STATE OF FLORIDA
COUNTY OF PINELLAS

Before me, the undersigned authority, personally appeared Trudy Capone, who being first duly sworn, deposes and says:

1.   My name is Trudy Capone, I am over the age of 18 years, and I make this statement on personal knowledge.

2.   On Monday, May 7, 2001, Kimberly Takacs ("KRT") interviewed me at my home. What follows is an accurate summary of our conversation:

KRT identified herself as an investigator and provided me with the proper identification. Not knowing what KRT was here to see me for, I said I would call the number on the business card to set up a time to meet and discuss the matter. Immediately KRT indicated that she was there regarding Terri Schiavo. I did indicate that my son advised me to not get involved if anything came up regarding me. I asked if KRT was here on the parents' side or Michael Schiavo's. KRT told me that she was here representing the parents of Terri and that she would really like to speak with me. I indicated that I loved Terri and felt so bad for her.

KRT asked me if Schiavo ever confided in me regarding Terri's care. I told her that Michael confided in me all the time about Terri. I did say, "I will tell you one thing. Michael never knew what Terri wanted. He never knew." He would say to me all the time, "I don't know what to do. I don't know that to do with her. I just don't know." I told KRT that if he said anything different he was a liar and that he said to me many times that he had no idea what her wishes were.

I told KRT that Michael and I were close, but were never romantically involved. I informed KRT that I felt the reason we were not romantically involved was because it was so close to settlement time, and I felt he was afraid of having it come out and did not need that at the time.

I tried to remember another girl that Michael was involved with. I told KRT that he was dating a nursing assistant with blonde hair. I am not sure if that was Cindy Brashers or not.

I stated that Michael went crazy on me when I ended our friendship because he was calling me so much and I needed more space. I informed KRT that one day at the hospital where I was working I was avoiding his calls, and a CNA informed Michael when he kept calling that I had run to McDonald's and was at lunch. Seemingly very upset, Michael told the CNA, " I know she's not at McDonald's, she would not eat there. You're lying. " I am something of a health food nut.

I have heard bits and pieces of what Cindi Brashers stated and it was all true and then some. I did not, however, hear the conversation between Brashers and the radio DJ that had been on the air. I have been trying to avoid listening to it all.

I informed KRT that Michael used to tell me that he would never give away Terri's car and how it was so special to him. I told her that as soon as he received his settlement he went out and purchased a gold Acura (I think that was the make) and drove it to my workplace just to show it to me. All he could talk about was his new car.

I told KRT that I knew that Michael and his new girlfriend/fiancee had a child and that another one was on the way. KRT asked me if I am sure of that, and I told her emphatically yes!! Michael talked about this child with staff members at Palm Gardens where Terri lived.

I stated that if Michael and I went anywhere, he would want to buy me expensive gifts. One day we were at the mall, and I saw a leather jacket and said how nice it was. Michael immediately said "Do you want it?" I told KRT that trial money was everything to him and that something happened to him once he received the settlement. He would say very mean things to me. When we ended our friendship, Michael Schiavo said to me, "You are too old, anyway." I told KRT I am approximately nine years older than he is.

KRT asked me about Terri when she cared for her; specifically if I ever observed any eye movement on Terri's behalf that would indicate Terri was following people who visited with her eyes and if she seems to really know what was going on. I told KRT "Absolutely! Yes, yes. Why do you think Michael would instruct us to give her medication when she was on her period?"

KRT asked me again about the earlier statement that I had made about Terri's wishes. I told KRT, "Kim, I swear to you he never knew what Terri wanted. He would confide in me all the time about how he did not know, and he would ask me what I thought he should do." Michael had no idea what Terri's wishes were, ▮▮▮▮▮▮▮▮ ▮▮▮▮▮▮▮▮▮▮▮▮▮▮▮ I told KRT that Michael used to tell me all the time that Terri's parents just don't want him to have the money and that they were mad because he was going to get it all and not them.

I told KRT that we would speak more formally regarding everything I had told her. I told KRT that I really just wanted to do what ws right. I told KRT to give the family my love and that I will tell KRT anything she wanted to know. She also said to KRT, "All I can do is tell you the truth. But again I will tell you Michael had no idea what Terri wanted. If it's one thing I do know it is that he never knew."

At that time KRT asked me to call and schedule a time to sit down and talk about more things. I indicated that as an RN I took an oath regarding patient confidentiality and did not want to jeopardize my career. I have no problem telling the truth about Michael Schiavo. I just feel that he was very sick and unstable and did not know what he would do.

Michael Schiavo got a job where I worked and sent me roses and made my job very difficult there every day. My co-workers would say to me, "Michael loves you, Trudy." In the beginning I felt like Michael really did love Terri, but after time passed he just wanted his own life and the money. Again before KRT left, I stated that if anything I know it is that Michael lied about Terri's wishes. At that time, KRT left, and I told her that I would call her to set up a time to discuss in more detail.

3   I have tried to avoid reading and listening about any of the Terri Schiavo case, but I feel guilty because I did not want to get involved. I should have sooner, and my heart is sick for the rest of the Schindler family.

FURTHER AFFIANT SAYETH NAUGHT.

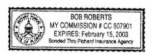

Trudy Capone, Affiant   5/9/01

The foregoing instrument was acknowledged before me this 9th day of May, 2001, by TRUDY CAPONE who produced a Florida driver's license as identification.

FL # C150-284-54-806-1   5/9/01

Notary Public

My commission expires:

STATE OF FLORIDA
COUNTY OF PINELLAS

AFFIDAVIT

BEFORE ME the undersigned authority personally appeared CAROLYN

JOHNSON who being first duly sworn deposes and says:

1. My name is Carolyn Johnson, I am over the age of 18 years and make

   this statement on personal information.

2. I used to work at Sabal Palms nursing home in Largo, for a period of

   about two years. I actually was employed by a nursing agency and

   was placed at Sabal Palms as a Certified Nursing Assistant (CNA). I

   believe the events related here occurred in about 1993.

3. During this assignment I took care of Terri Schiavo several times. The

   first time I saw her, my duties were being explained to me by the nurse

   on duty. Terri Schiavo was lying in bed. Another patient, also a

   young woman about the same age and in the same condition, was

   sitting up in a chair, with a drink cup and straw in front of her.

4. I asked why Terri was not up in a chair, too. I learned, as part of my

   training, that there was a family dispute and that the husband, as

   guardian, wanted no rehabilitation for Terri. This surprised me, as I

Page 1 of 3

did not think a guardian could go against a doctor's orders like that, but I was assured that a guardian could and that this guardian had gone against Terri's doctor's orders.

5. No one was allowed to just go in and see Terri. Michael had a visitors list. We all knew that we would lose our jobs if we did not do exactly what Michael said to do.

6. I remember seeing Michael Schiavo only once the entire time I worked at Sabal Palms, but we were all aware that Terri was not to be given any kind of rehabilitative help, per his instructions. Once, I wanted to put a cloth in Terri's hand to keep her hand from closing in on itself, but I was not permitted to do this, as Michael Schiavo considered that to be a form of rehabilitation.

7. This entire experience made me look hard at nursing homes. After about two years, I quit this job, because I was so disillusioned with the way Terri was treated. Someone somewhere along the way should have reported this.

FURTHER AFFIANT SAYETH NAUGHT.

Page 2 of 3

Carolyn Johnson

Carolyn Johnson, Affiant

Sworn to and subscribed before me this _28_ day of August, 2003, by

Carolyn Johnson who produced a Florida drivers license as identification.

Notary Public

My commission expires

Page 3 of 3

If you would like to learn more about the Terri Schiavo case, here are three websites with links to the legal records, medical information, timelines, bibliographies, and other resources:

http://www.miami.edu/ethics/schiavo_project.htm
http://abstractappeal.com/schiavo/infopage.html
http://www.terrisfight.org/